ANGUS CALDER

# *Byron*

Open University Press
*Milton Keynes · Philadelphia*

Open University Press
Open University Educational Enterprises Limited
12 Cofferidge Close
Stony Stratford
Milton Keynes MK11 1BY, England

*and*
242 Cherry Street
Philadelphia, PA 19106, USA

First Published 1987

**British Library Cataloguing in Publication Data**

Calder, Angus,
    Byron.—(Open guides to literature).
    1. Byron
    I. Title

    ISBN 0 335 15095 0
    ISBN 0 335 15086 1 Pbk

**Library of Congress Cataloging in Publication Data**
Calder, Angus.
    Byron.

    (Open guides to literature)
    1. Byron, George Gordon Byron, Baron, 1788–1824—
Criticism and interpretation. I. Title   II. Series.
PR4388.C33   1987      821′6.7      87–5764

    ISBN 0–335–15095–0

    ISBN 0–335–15086–1 (pbk.)

Series text design by Clarke Williams
Typeset by Quadra Associates Ltd, Oxford
Printed in Great Britain by J. W. Arrowsmith Ltd, Bristol

# Contents

# Series Editor's Preface

The intention of this series is to provide short introductory books about major writers, texts, and literary concepts for students of courses in Higher Education which substantially or wholly involve the study of Literature.

The series adopts a pedagogic approach and style similar to that of Open University Material for Literature courses. *Open Guides* aim to inculcate the reading 'skills' which many introductory books in the field tend, mistakenly, to assume that the reader already possesses. They are, in this sense, 'teacherly' texts, planned and written in a manner which will develop in the reader the confidence to undertake further independent study of the topic. They are 'open' in two senses. First, they offer a three-way tutorial exchange between the writer of the *Guide*, the text or texts in question, and the reader. They invite readers to join in an exploratory discussion of texts, concentrating on their key aspects and on the main problems which readers, coming to the texts for the first time, are likely to encounter. The flow of a *Guide* 'discourse' is established by putting questions for the reader to follow up in a tentative and searching spirit, guided by the writer's comments, but not dominated by an over-arching and single-mindedly-pursued argument or evaluation, which itself requires to be 'read'.

*Guides* are also 'open' in a second sense. They assume that literary texts are 'plural', that there is no end to interpretation, and that it is for the reader to undertake the pleasurable task of discovering meaning and value in such texts. *Guides* seek to provide, in compact form, such relevant biographical, historical and cultural information as bears upon the reading of the text, and they point the reader to a selection of the best available critical discussions of it. They are not in themselves concerned to propose, or to counter, particular readings of the texts, but rather to put *Guide* readers in a position to do that for themselves. Experienced travellers learn to dispense with guides, and so it should be for readers of this series.

This *Open Guide* to Byron's poetry is best studied in conjunction with *Selected Poems of Byron*, edited by Robin Skelton (Heinemann Educational Books). Page references in the *Guide* are to this edition.

# Acknowledgements

This book originates from material prepared for an Open University Course, A362 Romantic Poetry. Its shape and much of its detail evolved from discussion with colleagues on the Course Team and with our assessors. I am particularly grateful to Marilyn Butler, P. N. Furbank, Roberta Glave, Stewart Hamblin, Graham Martin, Susie Meikle, Brian Stone, Paul Townsend, Dennis Walder and Keith Whitlock. Also, to my then secretary, Allyson Moir.

But my involvement with Byron began with sheer delight, at school, over *The Vision of Judgement*. I was introduced to this poem by a teacher, Kenneth Richards, of whom I hope this book is not unworthy. I should like to dedicate to him whatever is my own in it (including the bits with which he disagrees).

Grateful acknowledgement is given to the National Portrait Gallery for permission to reproduce the photographs of Byron on pp. 12 and 13.

# Introduction

My aim in this book is to help readers to enjoy the poetry of Byron, and to assist you in 'placing' the writer, and the 'Byronism' with which his reputation was saddled, within the literary, cultural, social and political history of his day. The first aim takes precedence. It is, I believe, a mistake to separate literary texts from their 'background' and to assume that the latter is 'historical' and so somehow both more serious and more boring than mere works of imagination. And still worse to suggest that a work of poetical fiction such as Byron's *Vision of Judgement* or his *Don Juan* (or Dickens' *Bleak House*, or Tolstoy's *Anna Karenina*) is 'great' because, and in so far as, it measures up to this supposed 'background', or 'context' or 'historical' reality', squares with it, tells us 'truths' about this thing which exists outside itself.

In fact, literary texts (amongst which we may include works of vivid rapportage and biography and the livelier products of historiographical scholarship) are what primarily create for us that 'past' in our heads which we may or may not want to study, analytically, as historians do. And Byron, a dominant figure in the imaginations of many of his contemporaries, was as much the creator of 'history' in his own day as Wellington (and Rossini, and J. M. W. Turner). Reading *Don Juan* with gusto takes us directly into the centre of Byron's times and is as good a place as any to start understanding what they were like for his contemporaries and assessing their significance for us today.

However, I am not going to give much attention to the details of Byron's non-writing life. He has attracted a great many distinguished biographers – the twists and turns of his life and the enigmas surrounding his motivations are indeed extremely fascinating. But, to state what is obvious, they are not in themselves his poetry. While reviewers raved or raged, while lovers (male and female) came and went, while Shelley argued with him and Leigh

Hunt plagued him as a house guest, while political allies plotted, Byron withheld from the life which biographers love to record the very large proportion of his time which he devoted to producing narrative poems, plays and shorter poems in various modes using various voices. The life I'm concerned with here is the life alone with ink and paper to which his very large body of poetry testifies.

So great is Byron's output that this short book cannot possibly be comprehensive, or even refer to more than a fraction of it.

Please now read the following poems:

Several different styles of verse, in different genres, are represented. Perhaps even the most avid Byronist has never liked all these styles equally, and in dismissing this or that as bombastic or facile or trashy, you would always be in good company. On the other hand, Byron the lyricist, Byron the narrative poet, *Childe Harold*'s Byron, all have warm and cogent defenders. Please try to form your own first impression fearlessly. Enjoy what you can enjoy, don't be detained by what you can't, don't get bogged down.

Either before this reading, or after, you can refresh your memory of Byron's life, and acquaint yourself with a respectable judgement of his work, by digesting Robin Skelton's Introduction. Two caveats: it is rather important to realize that Professor Skelton is mistaken, on page 1, when he says that Byron's father was a *Scots* peer. Secondly, the statement on page 10 that Byron was 'a democrat by political conviction' is likewise untrue, and very seriously misleading – though, odd as it may seem, the word 'revolutionary' would be amply justifiable.

Byron's contemporaries read him fast, for pleasure. Whether or not they 'understood' what they read (and like many writers, Byron often complained of being misunderstood), they reacted strongly to it, for or against, sometimes for *and* against at once. I'm asking you to do likewise, and, as you read this book, to test your first impressions against the text and the arguments which I put to you.

Perhaps the most remarkable truth about Byron is that his verse has remained continuously 'controversial' since his first 'slim volume' to the present day. We're not reading some of it now in order to conform to received opinion, or to react against it. We have to take our own part in the hitherto ceaseless controversy.

# 1. Contexts

Byron was the most popular poet of an age when a new kind of narrative verse had become very popular. '. . . From 1813 until his death in 1824 he was, in all but two years, easily the best selling living poet. In four different years he outsold the combined works of the half dozen next most popular poets, living or dead'.[1]

And yet he had formidable rivals. In his dedicatory epistle to *Don Juan* (page 137) he denounces the poet Southey for attempting to 'engross' all the 'fame' available to British poets:

> Scott, Rogers, Campbell, Moore, and Crabbe, will try
> 'Gainst you the question with posterity.

He does not mention Wordsworth and Coleridge, whom 'posterity' has rated higher than any of these. But they had made no direct financial gain from the fashion for verse narrative which had brought vast sales to Byron and others. The success of Scott's *Lay of The Last Minstrel* in 1805 marked, the critic A. D. Harvey can argue, a more important break with the past than their *Lyrical Ballads*. '. . . Scott had tapped a market created by the psychological climate of the period which had been scarcely touched before . . . [He] did not merely take a literary tradition a step further, he created a new one from his intuitive response to the cultural environment of his age'.[2]

Byron was Scott's heir – as he put it himself, 'Sir Walter reigned before me' (*Don Juan*, Canto 11, stanza LVII). *Childe Harold* (1812), which established his reputation, was, as we shall see, an odd, unique poem; but Byron's verse narratives, which followed in spate, were in the genre which Scott had popularized.

What were the conditions under which *some* verse of the Romantic period sold, instantaneously, in great quantities?

The reading public in Britain had been expanding vastly. Growth can be measured by newspaper circulations (the poet Southey claimed in 1807 that some 250,000 people in England read the news everyday) and by circulation of serious periodicals reviewing new books. When the *Edinburgh Review* was founded in 1802, 800 copies only were printed. By 1818, it had a circulation of 14,000 – and each copy was probably read by an average of say a dozen people. The taste for reading had spread beyond a narrow élite through middle class sections of society, and the critics of the *Edinburgh Review* and its rivals zealously strove to educate and inform this public of *nouveaux riches* aggrandized by the wealth flowing into Britain, the greatest of imperial and commercial powers and now, through the 'revolution' in certain industries, becoming 'the workshop of the world'.[3] The new readership showed a taste not only for novels, still regarded as trivial by high minded persons, but for other novelties. 'This,' as Byron would remark in *Don Juan* (Canto 1, stanzas CXXVII and CXXXII), was 'the age of oddities let loose/where different talents (found) their different marts', and 'the patent age of new inventions'.

Book production was increasingly in the hands of 'four great publishers' – Longman and Murray in London, Constable and Blackwood in Edinburgh. These entrepreneurs, like their counterparts in the 'revolutionary' textile and engineering industries, planned boldly to increase profits through increased markets. High sales became the mark of poetic success. Very large financial rewards went with them. Scott got £600 (good money in those days) from Longman and Constable for his *Lay of the Last Minstrel*, which sold 21,300 copies in five years. Even today, when Britain's population is roughly four times greater, and every child is taught to read, such sales figures would be enough for a 'bestseller'. Delighted, the same publishers gave Scott £1,000 for *Marmion* (1808). By 1814 Moore could command an advance of £3,000 for his narrative *Lalla Rookh*. Yet like Scott, Moore was eclipsed by Byron. The growing public for literature was largely found among the leisured women of the prosperous middle classes.

Verse narrative remained an important literary genre for over a hundred years. By 1940, though, it was virtually dead. Despite very recent signs of some revival, it is now so little practised by poets, and so neglected by critics, that we have lost touch with the power which it had in its heyday. However, narrative was important to Wordsworth – see his 'Michael'. Coleridge's 'Ancient Mariner' and 'Christabel', though not at first widely read, had a powerful, even determining influence on the practice of Scott, Byron and other poets. Though Shelley and Keats did not produce 'bestsellers', they devoted much energy to verse narratives.

The form was capable of great variety. Tales of ordinary contemporary life related by Wordsworth and Crabbe are not superficially much like the medieval fables of Scott and Keats or the Eastern stories of Byron and Moore. But all had in common the fact that they broke away from 'classical' conventions such as had underpinned the eighteenth-century mode dubbed 'Augustanism'. This did not mean that they sprang up outside all former traditions of English verse. On the contrary, writers felt free to draw on many traditions: the ballads and broadsides of popular culture, the Renaissance verse narratives of Spenser and Ariosto, and the Greek and Roman tradition of epic. Post-Restoration 'classicism' in Britain had clung to concepts of 'high' and 'low' in style and subject-matter (though such individual Augustans as Pope and Fielding had not been much inhibited by them). War, a 'high' matter, required 'epic treatment. The new conventions of realism in *prose* fiction had helped to undermine such hierarchical notions, and now Wordsworth could write with dignity about the hitherto 'low' lives of common people, while, contrariwise, Scott could bring informality to the heroic topic of war, and Keats could project vivid sensuousness back into the classical world itself. But Keats was heavily reproved by Tory critics for so doing. Style was an ideological battleground. Romantic narratives which now seem to us at first sight clearly 'escapist' were, for their first readers, charged with political significance.

While arguing that a new freedom is the common basis of Romantic narrative, we can now usefully contrast two types. The tale of 'humble' life flourished with Crabbe; something very different under the wand of the 'Wizard of the North', Walter Scott. Byron learnt from both.

Crabbe was born in 1754, before Burns or Blake, and died in 1832, having outlived Byron. He was the son of revenue collector at Aldeburgh in Suffolk. He became a surgeon, but did not like his profession and at the age of 25 went to London to seek his fortune as an author. The day of the 'great publisher' had not dawned. Crabbe found fortune in a way typical of the eighteenth century. The statesman Burke became his 'patron', and arranged for his ordination as a clergyman and his appointment as chaplain to the Duke of Rutland. In 1783 Crabbe published *The Village*, to which *The Newspaper* followed in 1785. Then Crabbe was silent for 22 years. By 1807 the 'great publishers' were transforming the literary scene. From that year Crabbe began to reach the expanding reading public with his tales of Suffolk society. His heyday of popularity seems to have lasted till 1816. Scott and Wordsworth expressed their admiration, and the youthful Byron acclaimed him as 'nature's sternest painter, yet the best'.

Crabbe handles Pope's 'Augustan' medium, the decasyllabic

couplet, with great skill. But his content was far from 'classical'.
Here is the characteristic opening of one of his *Tales* (1812):

> To farmer Moss, in Langar Vale, came down
> His only daughter, from her school in town;
> A tender, timid maid! who knew not how
> To pass a pig-sty, or to face a cow . . .[4]

One characteristic of the poets of the era which we call
'Romantic' was their readiness to experiment with the idioms of
everyday speech, and this is clearly a contemporary of Burns and
Wordsworth, treating 'low' subject-matter in 'plain' diction.
Crabbe's sharp awareness of manners provides the humour which
at once raises this short passage above banality. He was also
contemporary with Jane Austen, who liked his work very much,
and his 'realism' in verse can hardly be separated conceptually from
that of 'realistic' prose fiction.[5]

I hope to convince you later that Byron's *Don Juan* also has to
be set alongside works of prose realism if we are to 'place' it
satisfactorily in literary history.

By contrast with Crabbe's, Scott's career was uniformly
spectacular from the publication of his first major work, *The
Minstrelsy of the Scottish Border*, a collection of folk song, in 1802,
when he was 31. More than any other writer, he *created* the new
reading public, showing it what it could and did want. After Byron
deposed him with the success of *Childe Harold*, Scott, anony-
mously, turned to prose fiction, and from 1814 'the author of
*Waverley*' poured forth novels in which all Europe delighted.

Scott was pivotal in the development of fiction. He brought to
the novel form a new perspective in which human character,
geographical setting, and history could be fused together. Besides
having a broad view of man-in-society, developed in Edinburgh, his
home town, during the eighteenth-century Enlightenment, he had a
passionate yearning to recover the past, not only from books and
manuscripts but also from the memories of old men and women.
His friendly contacts with ordinary people in town and country
helped make him the master of that new sense of history which
Stendhal and Balzac, Thackeray and Turgenev, and many others,
developed in prose fiction after him. Byron, too, loved Scott's
novels.

As a poet, also, Scott's role was very significant. Introduced by
a friend to Coleridge's still-unpublished 'Christabel', he seized with
delight on the new rhythmic freedom which the poem exemplified.
He was saturated in border balladry, and his *Lay of the Last
Minstrel* (1805) went back to the sixteenth-century social terrain

from which many ballads had sprung. Witchcraft, and possession by a fiend, added glamour to Scott's tale. But readers also encountered solid-seeming historical fact. The *Lay*, and Scott's copious footnotes to it, introduced the historically important blood-feud between Scotts and Kerrs, and included a typical raid by the English warden across the Border.

Metrical freedom and variety clinched the *Lay's* irresistible appeal. Scott popularized the technical discoveries of Wordsworth and Coleridge, and so prepared the way for wider public appreciation of those poets. Here is a small sample from the poem:

XXV

The sun had brighten'd Cheviot grey,
    The sun had brighten'd the Carter's side;
And soon beneath the rising day
    Smil'd Branksome towers and Teviot's tide.
The wild birds told their warbling tale,
    And waken'd every flower that blows;
And peeped forth the violet pale,
    And spread her breast the mountain rose.
And lovelier than the rose so red,
    Yet paler than the violet pale,
She early left her sleepless bed,
    The fairest maid of Teviotdale.


CXXVI

Why does fair Margaret so early awake,
    And don her kirtle so hastilie;
And the silken knots, which in hurry she would make,
    Why tremble her slender fingers to tie;
Why does she stop, and look often around,
    As she glides down the secret stair;
And why does she pat the shaggy blood-hound,
    As he rouses him up from his lair;
And, though she passes the postern alone,
Why is not the watchman's bugle blown?


CXXVII

The Ladye steps in doubt and dread,
Lest her watchful mother hear her tread;
The Ladye caresses the rough blood-hound,
Lest his voice should waken the castle round;
The watchman's bugle is not blown,
For he was her foster-father's son;
And she glides through the greenwood at dawn of light
To meet Baron Henry, her own true knight.[6]

The touches of apparent metrical carelessness – the third line of stanza XXVI is a salient example – are entirely deliberate. Scott had admired in 'Christabel' 'the singularly irregular structure of the stanzas, and the liberty which it allowed the author to adapt the sound to the sense'[7] – as he does in that 'trembling' line. Such liberty evokes the ballads strongly, but the elaborate stanza-form is not 'folk'.

Scott's second narrative triumph was *Marmion* (1808), a tale of war, love, treachery, and the supernatural set in early sixteenth-century Britain. The form of *Marmion* is devised so as to 'distance' the reader, to prevent what one might call *over*-romantic involvement. Each canto of the six is prefaced by an urbane introductory epistle. Contemporary allusions, conversational familiarities, thus intruded into the medieval narrative. The text, anyway, came swathed with learned footnotes. The first line of Canto First, 'Day set on Norham's castled steep', prompted Scott to a page-long note describing in plain prose the ruins of Norham and their history. Hence, though the tale itself is far-fetched, Scott's readers were less far from 'realism' than we might suppose. The same would apply later to Byron's. Byron was also a large-scale footnoter.

Scott's description of the battle of Flodden (1513), which provides the climax of *Marmion*, is both exciting and historically scrupulous. Rather than follow his invented personages into the thick of the fray, he makes us sit with some of them at a distance, seeing what they might see, guessing with them.

> At length the freshening western blast
> Aside the shroud of battle cast;
> And, first, the ridge of mingled spears
> Above the brightening cloud appears;
> And in the smoke the pennons flew,
> As in the storm the white sea-mew.
> Then mark'd they, dashing broad and far,
> The broken billows of the war,
> And plumed crests of chieftains brave,
> Floating like foam upon the wave;
>    But nought distinct they see:
> Wide rag'd the battle on the plain;
> Spears shook, and falchions flash'd amain;
> Fell England's arrow-flight like rain;
> Crests rose, and stoop'd, and rose again,
>    Wild and disorderly.
> Amid the scene of tumult, high
> They saw Lord Marmion's falcon fly:
> And stainless Tunstall's banner white,
> And Edmund Howard's lion bright,
> Still bear them bravely in the fight:
>    Although against them come,
> Of gallant Gordons many a one,

And many a stubborn Badenoch-man,
And many a rugged Border clan,
  With Huntly, and with Home.[8]

Technically, this stanza is less fresh and innovative than the verse of the *Lay*. The octosyllabic couplet is present as a kind of norm, and the way in which six-syllabled lines are used to vary pace and create fresh tension is perhaps somewhat mechanical. But the diction represents an important experiment. It will not strike us now as having novelty, because we are aware of so many later poets, including Byron, who made use of Scott's discovery that one could effectively mix medievalisms such as 'Of gallant Gordons many a one' with idioms inherited from Augustanism and with what one might call 'Lyrical Ballad' inventions. Look at the first few lines. 'The freshening western blast' is somewhat 'Augustan', and 'the shroud of battle' might have occurred to Pope. But the rapid switch between past and present tenses, and the sudden image of the white sea-mew, display the new Romantic freedom. Strong, direct verbs thrust the action along. 'Spears shook, and falchions flash'd amain.'

I think Scott's most impressive verse narrative is *The Lady of the Lake* (1810). Set in the Highlands in the reign of James V, its historical basis is that monarch's efforts to subdue Gaelic chiefs who were in effect little kings in their own right. Except for incidental songs and ballads, the whole poem uses octosyllabic couplets, with which Scott generates a narrative of remarkable suspense and extraordinary pace. In the stanza which follows, from Canto III, a highland chief, Roderick Dhu, has sent a follower out to rally the clan to oppose an invading Lowland army:

Speed, Malise, speed! the dun deer's hide
On fleeter foot was never tied.
Speed, Malise, speed! such cause of haste
Thine active sinews never braced.
Bend 'gainst the steepy hill thy breast,
Burst down like torrent from its crest;
With short and springing footstep pass
The trembling bog and false morass;
Across the brook like roebuck bound,
And thread the brake like questing hound;
The crag is high, the scaur is deep,
Yet shrink not from the desperate leap:
Parch'd are thy burning lips and brow,
Yet by the fountain pause not now;
Herald of battle, fate, and fear,
Stretch onward in they fleet career!
The wounded hind thou track'st not now,

Pursuest not maid through greenwood bough,
Nor pliest thou now thy flying pace,
With rivals in the mountain race;
But danger, death, and warrior deed,
Are in they course; speed, Malise, speed![9]

The poem contains several impressive sequences in which characters, as here, traverse difficult terrain at extraordinary speed, while Scott evokes the natural beauty of the areas through which they hurtle. This narrative established the Trossachs, not far from Glasgow, as a prime resort for tourism. I think it was able to do so partly because it is like a marvellous dream. In dreams we can fly, we can transfer rapidly from one place to another, and we meet ideal persons, like the eponymous 'lady' whom James V encounters living in exile on an island in Loch Lomond.

But we should not conflate 'Romanticism' with 'dreaming', or *The Lady of the Lake* with Mills and Boon. Scott was a wide-awake Tory. The three narratives which made him 'king' for a few years form a kind of trilogy harnessed to his right-wing patriotic objectives. Their aim can be seen as the reconciliation of all regions and classes of Britain at a period when the British nation-state was threatened by Napoleonic France. The *Lay* climaxes with a marriage between a Scott and a Kerr, joining representatives of two families bitterly at feud with each other. The English warden of the Border is present, enjoying the hospitality of the bride's Scottish mother. Since Catholicism is presented sympathetically (the poem actually ends with various warriors paying penance at Melrose Abbey), Scott's scheme of reconciliation includes the Catholic Irish who had revolted against British rule in 1798. *Marmion* strives much more blatantly to construct a sense of common national identity. A Scottish Earl dubs knight an Englishman who goes at once to help rout Scots at Flodden. The villainous but impressive Lord Marmion dies with a patriotic cry on his lips. The poem clearly implies that both English and Scots have heroic, chivalrous traditions in warfare, and these must now be jointly committed as fully as possible to the defeat of Napoleon. The *Lady* was explicitly intended to lay low at last the immemorial feud of Highlander and Lowlander. Though the state wins and Roderick dies, his people are represented as brave and generous like himself.

In these poems, Scott was able to reconcile historical and ideological contradictions which he understood and indeed felt very keenly – between Gael and Sassenach, England and Scotland, Protestant and Catholic. Also between rich and poor. In the sixteenth century, as he projects it, feudal loyalties bonded the classes together in harmony.

Byron's verse tales were equally saturated in ideology. But as we shall see when we look at *The Siege of Corinth*, his narratives tend to flaunt, even to fabricate, contradictions. Scott's stories create narrative suspense, resolved in restoration of order and harmony; Byron's tales also generate 'moral suspense', which he does not always fully resolve.

Why did romantic narrative appeal so much to the reading public? Here was have to distinguish between the popular 'Crabbe' type and the still more popular 'Scott' type. Crabbe's tales clearly had the same kind of attraction as did works of realistic prose fiction. The narratives of Scott and Byron, though not so far from prose realism as they may seem, didn't operate as 'simply' as that. They took their genteel, and commonly female, readers into remote times and places, to scenes of violence of kinds, and on a scale, which the comfortable middle class in Britain was not used to. They touched on, even harped on, 'dangerous topics': one use of narrative verse was that it gave harmless-seeming release to fantasies of illicit love.

But they also spread information about geography and history. Scott had a comprehensive vision of the past, and his footnotes anchored his narratives securely in it. (An 1810 edition of *The Lady of the Lake* contains 140 pages of closely printed prose footnotes to 290 pages of poem in single-column large type!) Byron's footnotes, too, were learned and copious. Romantic narrative verse had the very practical function of sustaining the British imagination in its struggle to control the new vistas opened up by imperial expansion and by wars fought simultaneously on several continents. Scott used a historical perspective in the construction of national identity. Byron expressed and promoted curiosity about geography. Scott's optimism about British society may have helped to pacify fears and doubts during wartime. As victory came, Byron's self-contradictory narratives, full of moral suspense, could be accepted.

Verse narrative, as an important genre, survived the triumph of the novel. Its collapse in our own time must in part be related to the rise of the cinema, a similar ideological battleground, which reconciles the claims of 'knowledge' and 'romance' – about war, say – even more successfully. Granted that narrative verse is no longer functional in our culture, do we agree that because it is obsolete, we need not, as readers and critics, bother with it? Do we accept the decline of Scott's reputation after about 1930, and the dubiety surrounding Byron's, as if they were irresistible 'natural' events?[10]

If you come to believe, as I do, that *The Lady of the Lake* is a remarkable poem, and that Byron's 'oriental' narratives have been underrated, how would we argue that these works are worthy of praise and study? Is it enough to say that they are suspenseful and 'colourful', and that their ideological content, once one notices it, is of great interest? Or does one have to inspect, perhaps even to dismantle, the whole system of ideas through which critics have come to agree that some works are great and important, others not? Such problems concern not only Scott and Byron, but also Crabbe and others in their day.

Recent studies of the 'popular culture' of our own times have drawn attention to the function of 'popular' literature in promoting, though commonly in disguised forms, attitudes and ideas of immediate political and social relevance. (Thus, Ian Fleming's 'Bond' novels can be related to the Cold War quite directly: less obviously, they seem to reassure readers that Britain is still a world power, such as it hasn't really been since the Suez crisis of 1956.) It could be argued that it is in the nature of popular literature that, as its vivifying context passes into 'history', the reasons for its being so popular need to be reconstructed – whereas writers like Wordsworth have engaged themes which have still persisting relevance.

You will find by the end of this book that I'm not at ease with the idea that 'timeless' Wordsworth is *necessarily* 'better' than 'topical' Byron. But you should consider, as we work through Byron, what, if anything, keeps his verse alive for you.

Is it, perhaps, precisely those elements which belong to his period – the ideological tensions, the topical allusions? To separate poetry from its so-called 'background' in history has been a disastrous, though very widespread, mistake. 'History' doesn't exist apart from men and women, including poets, or the books which they read, including books of poetry. The second-generation British 'Romantics', of whom Byron was one, were very well aware themselves that mystic isolation was not only undesirable, but impossible. As Marilyn Butler has put it, they rejected 'the way of solitude for the poet, which . . . they invariably represent as self-indulgent, narcissistic, cowardly or immoral'.[11] Poets weren't towering figures against a 'background', like some hermit saint positioned by a Renaissance painter against an empty Tuscan landscape. They were part of the life of their times, battered like shuttlecocks, swept like autumn leaves.

> Well, if I don't succeed, I *have* succeeded,
>     And that's enough; succeeded in my youth,
> The only time when much success is needed.
>     And my success produced what I in sooth
> Cared most about. It need not now be pleaded;
>     Whate'er it was, 'twas mine. I've paid, in truth,

Of late the penalty of such success,
But have not learned to wish it any less.

That suit in Chancery, which some persons plead
   In an appeal to the unborn, whom they,
In the faith of their procreative creed,
   Baptize posterity or future clay,
To me seems but a dubious kind of reed
   To lean on for support in any way,
Since odds are that posterity will know
No more of them than they of her, I trow.
(Byron, *Don Juan*, Canto 12, stanzas XVII–XVIII)[12]

Byron's speaker, characteristically, projects himself as being, along with his readers, involved in an irresistible flux of time and matter. The point is to live in the present – sensually, socially and politically. Reality cannot be 'transcended', but must be contended with, or accepted.

The lives of poets were as inseparable from the life-in-history of their own day as those of generals, industrial workers, abolitionists of slavery, or society ladies. Poetry and history still live together. As we read Byron now, he is part of our present-day history. 'Posterity', as Byron saw clearly, takes from the past only what it thinks it needs for its own contention with its own reality – in order to make its own history.

But Byron was exceptionally famous in his own day and so has a very special status in relation to *past* history. That relationship is expressed by the term 'Byronism'.

Please now look at the portrait of Byron on p. 12. We presume that the picture is 'like' the man in question, since the National Portrait Gallery owns it, and this institution claims to contain authentic representations of the great personages of the past. The NPG, furthermore, as our illustration on p. 13 shows you, holds another picture showing a similar man of the same name in Middle Eastern costume. There was a real Byron. He did look like that, and he was remarkably handsome. A Turkish potentate fell for him at once, when Byron was 21 and travelling in Albania. 'He said he was certain I was a man of birth because I had small ears, curling hair, & little white hands . . . he treated me like a child, sending me almonds & sugared sherbet, fruit & sweetmeats 20 times a day. – He begged me to visit him often, and at night when he more was at leisure' (To his mother, 12 November 1809).[13] The bi-sexual Byron was subjected to exceptional temptations by the readiness with which women, and men, were attracted to his pale brow and melancholy eyes.

Byron, George Gordon, 6th Baron (1813) *by R. Westall (© National Portrait Gallery, London).*

Portraits of Byron functioned, like icons, as objects of devotion. This is not an absurd simile. The free-thinking Russian poet Pushkin, one of the most important of many writers who were decisively influenced by Byron, wrote to his friend Vyazemsky on 7 April 1825: 'Today is the anniversary of Byron's death – I have ordered a mass this evening for the repose of his soul. My priest was astonished at my piety . . .'.[14] Many others felt a 'religious' emotion kindling in them as they thought of Byron, or looked at his painted or engraved effigy. For some, the nobility of his death as a warrior

Byron, George Gordon, 6th Baron, *by T. Phillips (© National Portrait Gallery, London).*

committed to Greek freedom eclipsed entirely his reputation for immorality. For others, his flagrant involvement in diabolic vices, his aura of wickedness, was itself a form of 'spiritual' potency. Had Byron died in, say, 1860, bald and fat, 'Byronism', paradoxically, might not have retained its grasp so long upon European consciousness. The icon of the young Byron, never supplanted by less dazzling images of him, conjured up an irresistible combination of beauty, pedigree, sexual challenge, revolutionary heroism – and *doom.* When his towering older contemporary Goethe celebrated the late Byron as 'Euphorion', child of Faust and of Helen of Troy, in his *Faust*, Part II, he made him leap towards the sun like Icarus, saying:

> The command
>   Is, sword in hand,
> To die: 'tis certain, once for all . . .
> Shall I from the distance view it?
> No! the fate be shared by me![15]

Nowadays, an image of Bogart or Monroe on the bedroom wall may serve as an icon in the same way, obliterating the real, suffering human being whose features it purloins and idealizes. Byron was not the first 'star' of his day. Throughout his intellectually formative years, the campaigns of Napoleon, from Iberia to Russia, gave people all over Europe a single object of attention. Napoleon's stylized image was instantly recognized everywhere. His stardom captivated liberals who forgot his hideous failings and thought devoutly of the force of progress which he represented, sweeping away the decayed monarchies and the mouldy feudalism of Europe. Byron followed in Napoleon's wake. 'Byronism' interacted with, fed upon, and complemented, the myth of Napoleon.

Byron's own attitude to Napoleon was complex. After British and allied troops entered Paris on 30th March 1814, Napoleon abdicated. Byron began an 'Ode to Napoleon Bonaparte' a few days later and his publisher, Murray, rushed it out within a week. This is a remarkable work and it is a pity that Skelton does not print it, since it illuminates Byron's tortured 'liberalism' very sharply. (Incidentally, there is a wonderful setting of it by Arnold Schoenberg, who has it declaimed by a speaker against an accompaniment by string quartet and piano. When the composer wrote this in 1944, the world was awaiting the fall of another militaristic, usurping would be world-conqueror – Adolf Hitler.) Byron's 'Ode' opens with an extraordinary mixture of regret and contempt:

>                               1
> 'Tis done – but yesterday a King!
>   And arm'd with Kings to strive –
> And now thou art a nameless thing
>   So abject – yet alive!
> Is this the man of thousand thrones,
> Who strew'd our Earth with hostile bones.
>   And can he thus survive?
> Since he, miscall'd the Morning Star,
> Nor man nor fiend hath fall'n so far.

2

Ill-minded man! Why scourge thy kind
  Who bow'd so low the knee?
By gazing on thyself grown blind,
  Thou taught'st the rest to see.
With might unquestion'd – power to save –
Thine only gift hath been the grave
  To those that worshipp'd thee;
Nor till thy fall could mortals guess
Ambition's less than littleness!

3

Thanks for that lesson – it will teach
  To after-warriors more
Than high Philosophy can preach,
  And vainly preached before.
That spell upon the minds of men
Breaks never to unite again,
  That led them to adore
Those Pagod things of sabre-sway,
With fronts of brass, and feet of clay.

The comparison with Lucifer, 'the Morning Star', suggests the awe
which Byron had felt for Napoleon. Byron elsewhere in his work
shows great respect for the Devil, seeing Milton's version of him in
*Paradise Lost* as heroic. He blames Napoleon for his despotism,
and for all the lives lost in his wars. Yet he also blames him for
giving in, for abdicating, rather than fighting to the last. Stanza 5 is
highly paradoxical, almost seeming to urge on Napoleon the line of
action which he followed when he broke out of exile on Elba, and
raised a new French army, only to be defeated at Waterloo.

5

The Desolator desolate!
  The Victor overthrown!
The Arbiter of other's fate
  A Suppliant for his own!
Is it some yet imperial hope
That with such change can calmly cope?
  Or dread of death alone?
To die a prince – or live a slave –
They choice is most ignobly brave!

Byron's ambivalence is further displayed in stanzas 9 and 10.

All Evil Spirit as thou art,
It is enough to grieve the heart,
  To see thine own unstrung:
To think that God's fair world hath been
The footstool of a thing so mean;
And Earth hath spilt her blood for him
Who thus can board his own!

Comparisons with famous dictators through history are the material of much of the 'Ode'. Byron intended it to end with Stanza 16, though since 1832 three additional stanzas have always been printed with it. Like his friend Shelley, Byron attached the highest symbolic value to the story of the Titan who rebelled against Jupiter on behalf of human kind.

### 16

Or like the thief of fire from heaven,
　Wilt though withstand the shock?
And share with him, the unforgiven,
　His vulture and his rock!
Foredoomed by God – by man accurst,
And that last act, though not thy worst,
　The very Fiend's arch mock:
He in his fall preserv'd pride,
And if a mortal, had as proudly died!

Napoleon's essential meanness ('that last act' refers to false gossip that he had had a casual affair just before he went into exile) means that he cannot measure up to Prometheus, or be seen like him as a martyr for liberty. Morally, Byron has to condemn Napoleon for his tyranny and cruelty. But on aesthetic grounds, he would have preferred him to go down fighting, like the greatest of all 'stars', Lucifer – to have perished with his 'Titanic' image intact.

On the way to his own final reputation as liberal martyr, Byron, as we have seen, looked back wrily at the days of his first stardom.

. . . I've paid, in truth,
Of late the penalty of such success,
But have not learned to wish it any less.

Like Napoleon or Monroe or John Lennon, he was the prisoner of his own fame. Unlike them, he could escape from it, eventually, into marvellously witty verse belying and mocking his public image.

What was the first 'star' image? It was that of a beautiful young man who had conquered the hearts of countless society women, and the beds of many, who had gone on to scandalize aristocratic 'society', and also the guardians of middle-class morality, by his treatment of his wife, and had then retreated to exile on the continent amid rumours of incest with his half-sister. He was identified with his own 'Byronic' heroes.

Thomas Love Peacock amused himself with that Byron in his novel *Nightmare Abbey* (1818), where 'Mr Cypress', a poet about to leave England, is made to say 'It is something to seek, Mr

Glowry. The mind is restless, and must persist in seeking, though to find is to be disappointed . . .' 'Scythrop' (Shelley) reproaches him for deserting his country in its hour of struggle against 'domestic enemies' (the Tory government), to which 'Cypress' responds:

> Sir, I have quarrelled with my wife; and a man who has quarrelled with his wife is absolved from all duty to his country . . . I have no hope for myself or for others. Our life is a false nature; it is not in the harmony of things; it is an all-blasting upas, whose root is earth, and whose leaves are the skies which rain their poison-dews upon mankind. We wither from our youth; we gasp with unslaked thirst for unattainable good; lured from the first to the last by phantoms – love, fame, ambition, avarice – all idle, and all ill – one meteor of many names, that vanishes in the smoke of death.[17]

Unless you have already read all or most of *Childe Harold* you are not in a position to judge whether or not Peacock's prose summary of its philosophizings and its mood are fair. But even readers who admire the long poem mostly agree that it lends itself to this kind of parodic treatment: 'sense of humour' is not its strong suit.

'Philosophizing' – not 'philosophy'. Byron was a deliberately unsystematic thinker, though he had a strong and original conception of man in relation to geographical space, to historical time and to the vaster universe. This cosmology was more simply expressed than Wordsworth's, and more drastic in its break with previous world-views (the existence of God, for instance, was left in doubt). It marked a major shift in European consciousness, though it did not create or express this alone, and, to name only two major precursors, Byron's debts to Gibbon, throughout, and to Goethe, in his last few years, were large.

But when Bertrand Russell included Byron in his *History of Western Philosophy* (originally published in 1946) it was less as a thinker than as an example for thought. '. . . His way of feeling and his outlook on life were transmitted and developed and transmuted until they became so widespread as to be factors in great events.' Russell saw Byron not only as an aristocratic rebel but as an exemplar for a cult of 'nationalism, Satanism, and hero-worship' which, Russell implied, had produced Nazism. 'Like many other prominent men, he was more important as a myth than as he really was'.[18]

Please now read in Skelton 'I would I were a careless child' (page 15), the extract from *The Island* on page 38 (Canto the Third, stanzas I–III) and that from *The Corsair* on page 32 (Canto the Third, stanzas XXI–XXIII). What do these suggest about Byronism?

DISCUSSION

The thrust of 'I would I were a careless child', sureley, seems anti-
social? It rejects settled countryside in favour of wild scenes, and
sets individual liberty against social convention.

It is a fluent piece of writing – you may well think if *over*-fluent
in places – from early in Byron's career. It begins with an evocation
of Scottish childhood which the speaker shares with his inventory,
though Byron, of course, hadn't dwelt in a 'Highland cave', but in
lodgings in Aberdeen. Typically of Byron, it then evokes the seas,
symbol of extra-social freedom, the domain of pirates. 'Saxon'
refers us to *English* society (as opposed to Gaelic), seen as
incompatible with such freedom. The third stanza might seem pure
'Mr Cypress' but for its subtly paradoxical play with the
connotations of dark and light. The rest of the poem, eloquently
voiced, confirms the speaker as one disenchanted with his position
in society, ready to 'fly' to the 'sullen glen', if only he had the wings
of a bird.

*The Island* is a long narrative based loosely on the famous
mutiny on the *Bounty*. The guilty mutineers, in this extract, have
'flown' to Tahiti – 'the isle they loved beyond their native shore' –
and are cornered there by righteous British pursuers. Stanza II
lines 13–14 and lines 23–24 are important for our purposes here.
The mutineers are fatalists, Cypress-like in their sense of doom.
And they are vicious. But they have a splendid animal tenacity –
'still the hunter's blood was on their horn' – and their lost cause is
half-identified with that, ultimately triumphant, of the ancient
Spartans who had died at Thermopylae defending Greece. In this
late poem Byron, committed to the cause of Greek freedom, invests
his hunted desperadoes for a few lines with some of the glamour of
libertarian struggle against tyranny.

Such shifts were not lost on his contemporaries. You may
remember that in my introduction, I questioned Skelton's description of Byron as a democrat. He was certainly a libertarian,
certainly a revolutionary. But he had no faith in 'the mob'. He was
an *aristocratic* revolutionary, of a type not uncommon in his
lifetime: he admired George Washington, the republican slave-
owner; and Pushkin's friends who led the abortive 'Decembrist'
coup in Russia in 1826 were, like Byron, 'liberals' conscious of their
aristocratic right to leadership.

Conrad, in *The Corsair*, whose 'real' name turns out to be Lara
in the sequel to that poem, is probably the most complete of
Byron's 'Byronic' heroes (though the verse tragedy *Manfred* offers a
different, but overlapping, projection of the 'type'). Conrad, the

pirate, is aristocratically aloof from his men, who nevertheless follow him out of awe, and out of self-interest, since he's a successful predator. His guilt kept secret – 'something he would not have seen' – his frightful scowl; these are a wish-fulfilment version of Byron's pose as he goes into exile (quite different from that accorded to him by Cruickshank in the cartoon reproduced on the cover of this book):

> There was a laughing Devil in his sneer,
> That raised emotions both of rage and fear;
> And where his frown of hatred darkly fell,
> Hope withering fled – and Mercy sighed farewell! . . .
>
> (lines 223–226)

> 11
> Yet was not Conrad thus by Nature sent
> To lead the guilty – guilt's worst instrument –
> His soul was changed, before his deeds had driven
> Him forth to war with man and forfeit heaven.
> Warped by the world in Disappointment's school,
> In words too wise, in conduct *there* a fool;
> Too firm to yield, and far too proud to stoop,
> Doomed by his very virtues for a dupe,
> He cursed those virtues as the cause of ill,
> And not the traitors who betrayed him still;
> Nor deemed that gifts bestowed on better men
> Had left him joy, and means to give again.
> Feared – shunned – belied – ere youth had lost her force.
> He hated man too much to feel remorse,
> And thought the voice of wrath a sacred call,
> To pay the injuries of some on all.
> He knew himself a villain – but he deemed
> The rest no better than the thing he seemed;
> And scorned the best as hypocrites who hid
> Those deeds the bolder spirit plainly did.
> He knew himself detested, but he knew
> The hearts that loathed him, crouched and dreaded too.
> Lone, wild, and strange, he stood alike exempt
> From all affection and from all contempt:
> His name could sadden, and his acts surprise;
> But they that feared him dared not to despise . . .
>
> (lines 249–74)[19]

The rumour of Byron's incest, probably based on fact, gave an apparent anchor in mundane reality to his otherwise inexplicably tortured heroes – and it became part of the public Byron-image to which his poems, despite his own disclaimers, were insatiably related by his readers.

Conrad's love for his woman, Medora, is his only soft trait. After a brave, and forlorn battle against his enemies, he escapes, but returns to his base to find Medora dead: 'the only living thing he could not hate'.

Bertrand Russell claimed that, by contrast with Nietzsche's, Byron's ethical vision was 'strictly conventional'. Russell missed the point that explicit ideas in poetry may be powerfully contradicted by implicit feeling. Look again at lines 7–17 on page 33 of Skelton or Canto the Third, stanzas XXI and XXII)

DISCUSSION

'He deserved his fate' seems conventional enough. A pirate somehow more guilty than other pirates – he has *secret* guilt – deserves his punishment. Yet surely the passage demands sympathy for those who *cannot believe* in that God who is supposed to deal out punishment? For those like Conrad who have no faith in a heaven, to lose 'all delight' on earth is to lose everything. The last four lines of stanza XXI implicitly praise the virtues of the stoic who can face the worst. Acclaim for stoicism was 'conventional' enough, but not in such a Christ-less context.

Conrad is a consummate man of action, and in section XXII he is associated with 'those that deepest feel', so that inwardly as well he has special capacity. It is human society's fault, we learn in XXIII, that he has been 'warp'd to wrong'. His relationship with Medora represented his essential 'softness'. Now, with her death, the 'rock' of his Byronic-Superman exterior and his inward 'lily' of fragrant purity are shattered simultaneously. This will not prevent him reappearing, as Lara, in the sequel, and leading the peasants of his ancestral homeland in an unsuccessful revolution.

I will have more to say about Byron's handling of the Byronic hero in relation to his *Vision of Judgement*. Some main features can now be summarized:

1 He is a rebel, essentially pure at heart, against the stifling conventions of society, like Jean-Jacques Rousseau, whose *Confessions* (published posthumously from 1782) Byron, like many Romantics, admired.
2 But unlike the pacific Rousseau, the Byronic hero, in his fullest development, is violently active, powerfully willed.
3 Fate will punish him for his sins. But there is a kind of animal majesty in his fight against fate. Doomed to be 'guilty' through no fault of his own, doomed to suffer, he struggles heroically against odds. (Manfred, in Byron's play, struggles against the entire spirit world.)
4 He is, politically, libertarian.

Byron's own death at Missolonghi transformed the urbane and genial author of *Don Juan* into a liberal martyr – and also conflated him once more with his earlier heroes.

So Byron and 'Byronism' must to some extent be identified. The historical actor, Lara–Byron, conspired, in the humourless spirit of 'Cypress', to create an image-cluster in which he participated with his own fictions. This was a best selling combination, internationally. It helped to foster a spirit of nationalistic and libertarian rebellion, and cults of leadership by exceptional men, in many parts of Europe.

Notice how the cult of the Great Sinner works to promote rebellion. The hero, in Byron's early fictions, is he who has burst out of conventional morality. This makes him not weaker, but stronger than other men. His active prowess, even if doomed, excels the routine courage of his conventional opponents and followers. The combination, in Byron's life and in some of his work, of notorious guilt, tragic courage, and rebellion against authority, was a potent cocktail which no other writer synthesized with quite the same force.

But – having acknowledged all this – was 'Byronism' Byron's own creation? In two ways, no. The role of scapegoat-*cum*–martyr was not just his own idea, deeply though his undoubted paranoia might conspire in his assumption of it. English society didn't have room for his kind of rebel, except as a best-selling literary monster. (The pop singer or film star, is not 'allowed to be himself'.) The imagination of the Regency reading public needed such a monster, it is clear.

How can I make that last statement with confidence? Because Byron did not *invent* the elements of Byronism. Only the way in which he put them together, and the context, were new.

The second half of the eighteenth century had produced – and they were not merely titillating, but *moving* in ways which can hardly grasp now – two new literary discourses of subversive potency. The cult of the feelings, of 'sentiment' and 'sensibility', was developed in Britain by the fiction-writers Lawrence Sterne (*Sentimental Journey, 1768*) and Henry Mackenzie (*Man of Feeling*, 1771). Goethe's *Sorrows of Young Werther* (1774), a much more powerful work than either, projected as its apparent hero an over-sensitive young man, alienated from the world, who kills himself. *Werther*, like the writings of Jean-Jacques Rousseau, had an impact on all literate Europe.

Parallel with 'sentiment' rose 'the Gothic' discourse. Horace Walpole's *Castle of Otranto* (1764) was the prototype Gothic, or 'gothick' story, and it is surely no coincidence that the archetypal

Byronic heroes, 'Manfred' and 'Conrad', have the same names as leading characters in this novel. Mrs Ann Radcliffe took the Gothick genre to a kind of peak in her novels of the 1790s. It involves violent action in remote, typically medieval, settings, and powerful figures of disturbing evil.

The drama of German proto-romanticism, with Goethe and Schiller, had thrown up elements of Byronism – Karl Moor in Schiller's *Robbers* (1781) was a particularly potent example, and through its influence on Scott, Wordsworth and Coleridge this play entered the mainstream of English writing. The tragic Karl, having contemplated suicide exclaims (in an early nineteenth-century translation), 'Shall I yield to misery the palm of victory over myself? – No! I will endure it! (*He flings the pistol away*). Misery shall blunt its edge against my pride! – Be my destiny fulfilled! (*It grows darker and darker*)'.[20]

Such plays owed a great deal to Shakespeare. Richard III, Edmund in *Lear*, Hamlet, Timon, Coriolanus fed into 'Byronism'. So did Milton's Satan, in *Paradise Lost*. Finally, there was the real-life Napoleon – man of destiny, man of guilt, man of doom to others, man doomed himself.

Now, the fact that various different existing, widely popular discourses – 'sentimental', 'Gothick', 'German', 'Shakespearian', 'Miltonic' – lay to hand for Byron to combine in a strong solution of his own highly specific paranoia doesn't in itself explain why the new mixture proved so intoxicating. Several social bases for Byronism's magnetic potency can be identified.

Firstly, the reading public was largely feminine. Rochester, in Charlotte Brontë's *Jane Eyre* (1847) represents the ambiguous appeal of the Byronic male – domineering, yet liberating, for many women of the Romantic period. Lady Eastlake, writing about the novel in the *Quarterly Review* soon after its publication averred that 'Mr Rochester is a man who deliberately and secretly seeks to violate the laws both of God and of man, and yet we will be bound half our lady readers are enchanted with him for a model of generosity and honour. . . . The popularity of *Jane Eyre* is proof how deeply the love of the illegitimate romance is planted in our nature'.[21] You might associate that appeal with the sexual attraction apparently radiated by Valentino's *Sheikh*, by Bogart, by Clint Eastwood, in our own century. Growing material comfort and security, expanding literacy, continued patriarchal domination of society, seem to create the conditions for a part-masochistic escapism.

Secondly, in Britain there was, despite the post-war recession, some scope for young men of fiery ambition, though increasing numbers meant increasing competition. In economically more stagnant countries (Germany, Spain, Russia, for instance) opportunities for talented aspirants were fewer, though population was everywhere increasing. Such disproportion between talent and opportunity had been a major factor in the American Revolution of 1776, and played its part in subsequent revolutions and nationalist movements. Byron was a model for disenchanted youth. Thus, his cult in Russia was associated with the projection in fiction of 'superfluous men', youngsters unable to use their imagination, intellect, and feelings in a rigidly autocratic, economically sluggish, society. In Lermontov's great novel *A Hero of Our Time* (1839–40) one Byronic poseur, a cold man, kills in a duel another Byronist, a man of pretended deep feeling.

This illustrates the complexity of Byronism – its breadth of appeal, its capacity for self-contradiction. It may seem obtuse of Russell to have accused Byron, arch-libertarian, arch-internationalist, of contributing to the development of Nazism – yet his mutineers in *The Island* do live and die by values not incompatible with that disgusting creed.

'Byronism' has to be clarified before we can see Byron's poetry as it is – in some places 'Byronic', wholeheartedly so, in others non-'Byronic' and even, deliberately, anti-'Byronic'.

# 2. Byronic narrative: *The Siege of Corinth* and *The Prisoner of Chillon*

*The Siege of Corinth* was published, with another verse tale, *Parisina*, in February 1816. Jerome J. McGann, the latest editor of Byron's works, believes that Byron had begun it as early as 1812 and patched it together at various times between then and 1815. The first 45 lines as printed by Skelton, and always so printed since 1832, were left out of early editions because neither Byron nor his publisher was sure that they worked. McGann remarks severely that 'there is no editorial justification for including the lines in the poem'.[1]

In the *Siege*, Byron deals with an historical event which took place in 1815, during a war between Ottoman Turks and Venice. His tale is drawn partly from *A Compleat History of the Turks* published in 1719, and partly from moral traditions which he had heard in Corinth in 1810. His imagination supplied the rest. Please now re-read the poem. As you do so, please consider:

1 The role and character of the Byronic hero, Alp.
2 The poem's ideology. What is its view of the Christian and Islamic religions? What is it saying about 'Freedom'?
3 Byron's versification. He establishes as his basic measure, the octosyllabic couplet which he had, so to speak, inherited from Scott, but he departs from it strikingly in several passages. Do his 'variations' seem to you effective?

DISCUSSION

The *Siege* isn't wholly typical of Byron's short verse narratives, which are, in fact, very varied in form and atmosphere. Alp isn't such a 'complete' or striking example of the Byronic hero as Conrad. Nor so attractive. He is a 'renegade' fighting for the Turks, whose rule over Greece Byron detested, and wanted his readers to detest. Furthermore, Alp has deserted *Venice*, a proud republic which had represented a tradition of civic freedom, to serve the Ottoman Sultan. The Turks, 'to *Greece* and *Venice* equal foes', represent despotism down the millennia.

Whereas Conrad, the Corsair, dominates a whole narrative, Alp's fate, as the poem's title suggests, is less important than the fate of the city. Note also that Conrad is projected for us in iambic pentameters, weighty, even 'classical'; Alp is a mere creature of octosyllabics, which scale him down. That said, Alp does generate, until the last third of the poem, the kind of 'moral suspense' which, in Chapter 1, I put forward as characteristic of 'Byronic' narrative. Like other Byronic heroes, he has been calumniated in his homeland. We 'suspend' judgement because both his alleged crime and the degree of his guilt – or innocence – are left vague (lines 129–34). We infer from section VII that he is (like Conrad) essentially *soft* by nature – though he is now carapaced in vengeful violence. And, as with Conrad and others of the type, we are drawn into complicity with his feelings: his presentation is not purely 'external'.

McGann in his notes describes lines 242–494 as 'Alp's Meditation'. There is, I hope you'll agree, a shift of viewpoint from narrative omniscience towards a more personal perspective. Byron handles the transition skilfully. Section XI has a softer, more 'inward' (more 'meditative') tone than its predecessors. It exposes a contrast between Byron and Wordsworth. Byron does not, here – or, as a rule, elsewhere – fuse Man with God via Nature. The 'mighty waters' for him do *not* 'roar evermore' as in Wordsworth's 'Immortality Ode', with the implication that we share in their eternity. He yearns to be one with the 'eternal' stars, but can't be. Nature is tranquil, 'Byronic man' is ill at ease. The Muezzin's strain represents his forebodings: we yearn, we die, and that, if we don't believe in heaven, is all.

Alp's companions *do* have faith in the concrete delights of Islamic paradise; he *doesn't*. Byron draws us into sympathy with the renegade, the outsider. If 'we' in 1816 had identified with Alp – and probably many readers did so – 'we' would have found ourselves temporarily at odds with all safe and settled religion and morality. We'd have been tempted to do so by a kind of psychic pride: we would rather claim affinity with the brave loner, the 'lion', than with the 'jackals'. Alp has specially strong feelings (lines 320–231), which are beyond his companions' comprehension.

Section XIV is a key passage in the poem, which introduces intellectual, 'ideological' suspense to join our moral suspense over Alp. We're not quite sure whether the thoughts it contains are narrator's, or hero's, or both, and these thoughts are extremely disturbing. 'Tyrant', 'slave' – and everything human – are 'swept away' by time. Freedom is symbolized by the 'eternal' snow on the brow of Delphi, site of the Oracle of ancient, *free* Greece: it seems part of the 'nature' from which Byronic man is alienated irrevocably. There is a contest between fatalistic pessimism – the pure mountain snow is like a 'shroud' – and libertarian activism, which hopes for better days when the spirit of the Spartans at Thermopylae will reawaken. (They all *died*, but they saved Greece.) This contest is not really resolved by section XV, where Alp (the thoughts are certainly his now) compares his own dismal role with that of past and future heroes of liberty. What can man do? In XVI nature seems 'changeless', the moon is described as 'powerless' as well as 'heedless'.

Lines 454–78 have special interest. Byron insisted on including this sensational passage, against the advice of Gifford, an older poet who acted as his mentor. The word 'cynical' derives from the Greek for 'dog', and a more 'cynical' passage is hard to imagine. Byron, shockingly, uses a 'light' rhythm: the lilt suggests a *danse macabre*, dance of death. The reader is called up jeeringly to see the dogs' appetites as like his own – 'As ye peel the fig when its fruit is fresh.' Robert F. Gleckner, argues that 'the sickening scene in all its crudeness is merely a hyperbole for human life . . .' and that 'the purity of Eden' is 'being re-established with the end of fallen bestial man'.[2] Perhaps Gleckner goes too far, but lines 491–94 help his case. The narrative has insinuated that the value of any and all human activity is debatable, and its savage insistence here on the vulnerability and transience of flesh forces the thought home. The creatures of nature, these dogs, are indifferent to human 'Fame' and 'Honour' (section XVII).

The contrast between the skittish skip of Byron's metre and the grim images and thoughts creates a special kind of intensity. I think it effectively mimics the antithesis between human endeavour – frail and pointless – and the basis on which it performs – 'the weltering field of the tombless dead'.

Byron's departures from the octosyllabic norm of the poem are here at their most extreme. That norm is represented by the completely regular opening couplet of stanza XVI, which is neatly iambic, with four stresses. Though line 461 still has four stresses, it has eleven syllables, and its first three feet are anapaestic. But the previous line is metrically almost unclassifiable. Of its ten syllables, five, it seems to me, have to be stressed, including three in succession – 'white tusks crunched'. Byron uses the freedom, which, *via* Scott's *Lay* (see p. 5) he had inherited from Coleridge, to very striking effect indeed here.

Having drawn us, through our identifications with Alp, very deep into 'Byronic' fatalism, the narration, from line 495, pulls away from him. When Alp encounters Francesca (or rather, as we infer later, her ghost), his violent aims are exposed as inherently futile. He can only reach his beloved, he thinks (lines 581–82), by helping to massacre her fellow-Christians: how could happiness in some 'lovely spot' be born from such horror? In fact, his 'deep interminable pride' (line 654), overwhelming all softer feelings, makes him incapable of happiness, and, we must feel, unworthy of it. In this poem, *moral* suspense is effectually resolved – after line 677, Alp's fate is settled, in terms we must see as just. But *ideological* contradictions remain unresolved. We return from Alp to the poem's overarching themes.

Let's now go back to section I. Corinth symbolizes political Freedom – both that won by the valiant resistance of ancient Greece to Persia and the freedom which Byron hoped that modern Greeks would struggle to regain. Timoleon's name (line 59) makes the connotation of 'Freedom' more specific. It isn't just 'national independence', as when we say that an African country 'gained freedom' from Britain in the 1960s though it has since been ruled by dictators. 'Freedom' for Byron implies 'civil rights'. When his brother tried to rule as a tyrant in Corinth, the ancient Greek statesman Timoleon had him killed.

But 'ideological suspense', is there from the outset. The apparent serenity of present-day Corinth is in contradiction with the city's bloody history. Freedom and death are evoked together in lines 58–70. The image of dead piled high haunts the rest of the poem, as does the contest displayed, as we've seen, in 'Alp's mediation' between Freedom/Activism and Time/Fatalism.

It is clear that neither Christian nor Turk, in the poem, adequately embodies Freedom. The 'glory' of the Moslem commander Coumourgi is invoked, without irony, in section V. In section XXV, the courage of old Minotti is vividly presented; unyielding bravery against odds is one of the *positive* Byronic virtues. But see how Byron refuses to commit his readers straightforwardly to the Christian cause. Line 793 can be read as 'spoken' from a Muslim point of view, and by the end of the section the carnage which Minotti executes out of a spirit of revenge begins to seem horrible – not only that, but futile, mocked by Death and Time. The church into which they retreat cannot save the Christians. Byron is solemnly impious in the play which he makes with the Madonna, 'painted in heavenly hues', who smiles inanely upon the slaughter.

The image of dead piled upon dead recurs in its most macabre form in section XXXI. And if at this point Minotti, defending Corinth, represents Freedom, all Freedom can do is – blow everything up. The town, symbol of Freedom, is 'shatter'd', though the hills – indifferent nature – are 'unrent'. The narration in the last section becomes almost jeering (lines 1041–42). Objectively – set against Time and Death – freemen and slaves, Christians and Turks, are not really different. The work which the dogs did was nothing to this; and the dogs duly flee abashed. Man asserts himself against nature here, but only in colossal self-destruction. Minotti's firework display is a fatalistic outburst against fate.

The poem ends with 'ideological suspense' not *resolved* but emphasized. There is irreconcilable discord between the survival of Corinth, celebrated in section I, and the cataclysm of XXVIII. Hence, I think, the poem can still disturb us.

Please now read the poem 'Darkness' (page 25). How does its vision relate to that of *The Siege*?


DISCUSSION

Byron here produces a scenario for the *ultimate* disaster movie! Even John Martin 1789–1854), whose huge canvasses depicting such cosmic horrors as 'The Deluge' were popular in Byron's day, never projected a vision so appalling. The poem, though written in a graver metre, suggests a grim relish in its author akin to the last section of *The Siege*, and this inhibits us from taking its vision 'seriously'. The vipers, for instance, which twine themselves around men and are slain for food, bring in a touch of hyperbole-over-and-above-hyperbole, as does the one dog which inexplicably remains devoted. Nevertheless, 'Darkness' bears a significant relationship to *The Siege* and *The Prisoner of Chillon*. Their author, we learn from it, could boldly imagine a situation in which all human aspiration would come to nothing, and there was no God to intervene.

There had been powerful visions of horror before his, of course. Dante's *Inferno*, the Hell of Milton's *Paradise Lost*, certainly helped to direct his imagination, and from both poems he could have gathered many hints as to how to handle extreme psychological states, in relation to extreme physical circumstances. Nevertheless, *The Prisoner of Chillon* – a much more restrained poem than *The Siege* – even, in its strange way, one which reaches a 'resolution' – does mark a leap which, with Byron, the Western imagination took. Humankind had somehow to live with itself in a Godless universe.

*The Prisoner of Chillon* is a product of the early period of Byron's exile. For the Romantics, Switzerland was strongly associated with political and intellectual liberty. William Tell had become the symbol of the medieval struggle for independence of the Swiss cantons, which had then played a crucial role in the sixteenth-century Protestant Reformation. More recently, Switzerland had been the birthplace of the intellectual rebel Jean-Jacques Rousseau; the great French free-thinker Voltaire had lived prudently close to the Swiss border; and Edward Gibbon, debunker of Christian history, had found a home on the shores of Lake Geneva, 'Lac Leman'.

By these shores Byron took a villa in 1816. He at once, with Shelley, as his companion, toured nearby scenery associated with Rousseau. He sent his publisher a sprig of Gibbon's acacia and some rose-leaves from his garden. He was fascinated by the Castle of Chillon; after visiting it in June 1816, he swiftly composed *The Prisoner of Chillon*, prompted by the story of François Bonnivard (1496–1570), a sixteenth-century defender of the liberty of Geneva against its tyrant ruler, the Duke of Savoy. Bonnivard had been immured in the castle without trial from 1530 to 1536.

But when he wrote his narrative Byron knew little of the real Bonnivard, who had emerged from Chillon to find Geneva a free republic with a Reformed Church. There is a discrepancy between the *Prisoner* and the 'Sonnet on Chillon' which prefaced it, but which was composed later.

> Eternal Spirit of the chainless Mind!
>    Brightest in dungeons, Liberty! thou art,
>    For there thy habitation is the heart –
> The heart which love of thee alone can bind;
> And when thy sons to fetters are consign'ds –
>    To fetters, and the damp vault's dayless gloom,
>    Their country conquers with their martyrdom,
> And Freedom's fame finds wings on every wind.
> Chillon! thy prison is a holy place,
>    And thy sad floor an altar – for 'twas trod,
> Until his very steps have left a trace
>    Worn, as if thy cold pavement were a sod,
> By Bonnivard! May none those marks efface!
>    For they appeal from tyranny to God.[3]

In this sonnet, Chillon, like Corinth, becomes a holy shrine of civic
Freedom. Bonnivard is quite unambiguously a martyr for Freedom,
which 'conquers' through such martyrdoms. But we will misread
the *Prisoner* if we try to accommodate it to the rhetoric of the
sonnet. Please now read the poem. What is it really about? If not
'martyrdom for Freedom', what?

## DISCUSSION

You may have concluded that it's merely a deft exercise in the
projection of intense psychological states. Bernard Blackstone calls
it 'a very superior tear-jerker'.[4] But other critics have found more in
it. Robert F. Gleckner claims that the poem chronicles 'the slow
decay of the human mind in the dungeon of its being'.[5] The speaker
'grows for the poet (and the reader) into a microcosm of mankind'.

Before I attempt my own reading of the poem, I'll pause to
admire the skill of its composition. Byron establishes at the outset a
norm: a four-foot octosyllabic line, which he will generally use in
couplets, with practised assurance. At once, though, he establishes
his freedom – to break the line in two (lines 2–3), to rhyme in
quatrains, to reduce the number of syllables to seven while
retaining four feet (lines 18–20) or dropping (as I hear it) to three
(line 19). The stresses wander freely, and the combination of
control and freedom is crucial in defining the speaker's tone. The
poem's 'voice' is grave and authoritative – not that of a neurotic,
but of a man commanding respect. But the slitherings of the stresses
from line to line serve to emphasize his mental anguish, to make us
feel how hard-won his control must be.

Note also the simplicity of the diction. There are striking
phrases – 'rusted with a vile repose' is magnificent, with its almost
paradoxical combination of adjective with noun. But there is
nothing flamboyant, sensational, conventionally 'poetic' in the
diction. The speaker's experience is enough in itself to move us,
conveyed directly, often in blunt monosyllables (lines 1, 5, 8, 17,
18, 21, 26).

Byron may have been remembering Coleridge's 'Ancient
Mariner'. His diction is more restrained than Coleridge's, without
archaisms or sensational effects like 'white as leprosy', but aspiring
to a similar ballad-like impact. As with the 'Mariner', we are in the
grip of a story-teller with a tale to freeze our blood, a story-teller
who may be mad.

Byron had been brought up in Scotland till the age of 10, under
the charge of Calvinist nurses. He understood the central drama of

Calvinist theology, such as had developed and flourished in Geneva. Man, individually, starkly confronts an omnipotent Maker who has already decided, from all eternity, whether he is damned or sainted. Priestcraft and wishfulness and good works are alike powerless to redeem a soul. Bonnivard's imprisonment had preceded Calvin's arrival in Geneva (1536). However, the specific situation of the historical Bonnivard, even the nature of his religious beliefs, are irrelevant to this poem. Byron uses, we might say, the Calvinist conception of the lonely soul, but he does not re-enact the Calvinist drama in Christian terms. What is at issue is individual man's relationship to the material universe, which has replaced God, in Byron's cosmology, as the aloof presence dominating his destiny. Time, matter, mock man's enterprises and aspirations.

The real Bonnivard had only two brothers, and neither was imprisoned with him. But seven is a number which traditionallay carries magical connotations; it helps cast a spell. There are seven brothers, seven pillars. The link which we cannot help making between these implies that somehow the brothers support the very dungeons in which three are imprisoned. The speaker of the poem dwells in the prison of his own 'lineage'.

Their struggle has been against – what? Its name is general – 'Persecution': a term which applies both to the real torments dealt out by the Inquisition or the Nazis and to the blows imagined by a paranoiac. We are not equipped by the speaker of this poem with means of judging in his own case. We must take it on trust that he is persecuted unjustly.

The youngest brother is a man of 'feeling', whose tears flow 'like mountain rills'. The other is a man of action, 'form'd to combat with his kind'. They represent different facets of the Byronic hero which in Conrad or Alp were combined. The eldest, the speaker, represents the brooding consciousness of *Homo Byronicus*, his obsession with evil done to him by 'Persecution'. But no *guilt* haunts him – that element is missing. As in paranoia, all guilt is thrust on to the Persecutors. And what Persecution they have devised!

The colossal – and exaggerated – depth attributed to 'Lake Leman' intensifies the horror, in section VI, of the notion of a 'double dungeon'. The violence of the water has on occasion been such that

. . . the very rock hath rock'd,
And I have felt it shake, unshock'd . . .

The simplicity of the verbal effect here – it is onomatopoeic – is in key with the poem's overall restraint; the thud of the waters is straightforwardly mimicked by the stark stabs of repeated, then alliterating words. But the speaker's state of mind is not so simple: he would, he says, have welcomed death as setting him 'free'.

Note that the freedom his brother misses, in section VII, is purely personal freedom, enjoyed by himself on 'the steep mountain's side' apart from society. Milton had written nearly two centuries before of 'The Mountain Nymph, Sweet Liberty', and there was a strong and obvious connection for the Romantics to draw, following Rousseau, between the freedom from constraint of the mountain shepherd or hunter and the political libertarianism which such conditions of life in fact engendered in some parts of the world. But the freedom evoked here is actually remote from the ideal of civic liberty, of a free *society*, for which the historical Bonnivard seemed to have suffered. The opposites evoked in this section are: free movement/chains, fresh air/close confinement, 'natural' soil/'flat and turfless earth'. Consider how different the effect would have been had the brother yearned for the society of his peers, had Bonnivard asked for a civic funeral. The brother is no more a social being than Conrad or Alp – his very lack of a *name* helps to detach him from human context.

The younger brother, the man of feeling, does at least grieve 'for those he left behind'. But his social bearings also are left vague – there is no mention, for instance, of a loved woman. The Prisoner retains his faith in God, but this does not save him from the utter despair projected in section IX, a key stanza. 'Persecution' has reached its climax – and so has paranoia. Let us consider the jailers for a moment. In line 159 'they coldly laugh'd'. Otherwise, they have had no personality, no presence in the poem. Yet the Prisoner must clearly have been fed. We must infer that some compassion operated when he was not chained up again. Of the human nature of his jailers he gives no acknowledgement; they remain 'Persecution', an abstraction.

You may be thinking by now that I am systematically avoiding the obvious level on which the poem operates. It invites us (you might say) to sympathize with the sufferings of a martyr for a cause. It enhances, through the deaths of his brothers, the pathos of his predicament, and the pain of bereavement explains his morbid state of mind. Basically, you might aver, the poem elicits indignation against Persecution; the Prisoner stands for all who have thus been treated in

> . . . many a thousand years,
> Since man first pent his fellow men
> Like brutes within an iron den . . .

Need interpretation go beyond saying that this poem is indeed a 'tear-jerker', written for a cause which Byron thought good?

Well, you'd have much sense on your side. But you'd also be evading our implicit question: what 'cause' is in the Prisoner's mind? The answer must be, no cause at all – merely personal loss, personal suffering. The Prisoner is obsessed with his own states of mind.

Byron's imagination was hardly outraging common likelihood when it conceived that a man left alone in such circumstances might become entirely self-obsessed. To break a man's spirit is often the aim of those who imprison, rather than execute, an enemy, and experience proves that it can be done. Be that as it may, it is not the prisoner's martyrdom for a cause that gives the poem its real interest – the sonnet says all that needs to be said about that. It is his descent into utter alienation from the human world and the natural parameters which normal humans take for granted, as evidenced in lines 231–50. The line 'Among the stones I stood a stone' is particularly significant. Whatever 'faith' prevents his suicide, the prisoner now has no sense of himself as an individual 'soul'. He is reduced to nihilism, he feels himself to be part of a material universe indifferent to such human conceptions of 'time' and 'good' and 'crime'. All three conceptions are necessary to a Christian defining his relationship with God, which exists in time and involves sin and virtue. The Prisoner, 'the mate of misery', has moved beyond Christianity.

What follows is his limited reintegration with life outside himself, not through human society, nor through prayer, but through a kind of flirtation with nature. A bird *seems* to sing only for the Prisoner, a bird which *seems*, like him, to be bereft of primal companionship. This is enough to bring him 'back to feel and think'. Though the bird proves not to be a kind of lover, nor his brother's soul, merely a 'mortal' bird which flies away, it has reintroduced him to a sense of distinction, between Paradise and prison, between sun and cloud.

But he does not go on to yearn for Paradise and sun. He no longer wishes to escape. His 'spirit', so far as human affairs are concerned, *is* broken. Without *kindred*, the world will be merely 'a wider prison' to him. We see clearly that he represents now not a cause, which would be of relevance to all human beings, but a 'race'. He cannot see beyond his dead family. The rest of humanity doesn't offer any promise at all.

In Coleridge's poem, the despairing Mariner, 'Alone on a wide sea', is brought back to Christian faith by a vision of 'happy living things'; a 'spring of love' gushes from his heart, his Albatross falls

from his neck: he can pray. This experience produces the poem's
'moral', to use an appropriately old-fashioned term:

> He prayeth best, who loveth best
> All things both great and small;
> For the dear God who loveth us,
> He made and loveth all.

To a Calvinist, or to anyone who has been bred to a Calvinist
sensibility without necessarily sharing Calvinist faith or theology,
these lines must seem preposterous nonsense. God does not love
'all'; he damns most to perdition, as he has every right to do. The
'carnal' universe is to be valued as dust compared to the exaltation
of God's saints, the saved; if one does not believe in salvation, it still
seems at best indifferent, remote.

Byron's Prisoner is, so to speak, offered a Coleridgean, or
Wordsworthian, escape into love. He rejects it – not on theological
grounds, but with a plausible psychological reflex. The world,
offering specious hope of love, brings tears. Its bright delusions are
more than he can bear. The isle with its 'three tall trees' is the centre
of a natural scene full of activity, such as Wordsworth had evoked
in his 'Immortality Ode'; and it hints at the three crosses at
Gethsemane, the Christian promise of our redemption through
Christ's sufferings as a living man. The Prisoner turns from this,
from the fishes, from the eagle. He 'learns to love despair'. Only the
creatures which live with him in prison – spiders and mice – attract
his affection. 'My very chains and I grew friends.'

He does regain his 'freedom'. Though he has ignored society,
society nevertheless sends men to 'free' him. But what is the content
of 'Freedom'? For the active brother, it was solipsistic action, alone
on the mountain-side. For the Prisoner himself – what? We are left
with nothing but the sense that physical freedom has become
unimportant; the whole earth will from now on be his prison.

We can be certain that Byron often remembered famous lines
from *Paradise Lost*, by John Milton, whose consciousness had
struggled heretically inside and out of the Calvinist vision of life,
and whose Satan so impressed many Romantics. Cast out of
Heaven, Milton's Satan heroically uprears himself from the
burning lake where he is chained, and heroically accepts Hell as his
home:

> The mind is its own place, and in itself
> Can make a Heaven of Hell, a Hell of Heaven.
> (Book I, lines 254–55)

The Prisoner's mind, surely, is 'its own place'. It reconciles itself to
imprisonment and creates a kind of Peaceable Kingdom in the

dungeon, where, like Adam with the beasts before the Fall, he has 'power to kill' but lives in friendship with all things.

Unlike Coleridge, Byron offers no 'moral' (though his later sonnet gives this narrative a specious moral 'frame'). We are left with a statement of psychological fact – that the human mind can, and perhaps must, adjust to the most extreme privations – and a symbolic vision of man-in-cosmos which relates to the Calvinist vision, but virtually does without God. The individual is alone. He is trapped in his own consciousness, and cannot trust the 'seeming' blandishments of the apparently joyous natural world. The Prisoner's 'mind is its own place' – he exercises, effectively, as much 'free will' in jail as in the world, that wider prison.

Must we assume that Byron himself ventriloquizes through the Prisoner? One striking feature of the speaker's consciousness, his obsession with his own lineage, may be related to Byron's own sense of belonging to a doomed aristocratic lineage, the violent 'race' of Byrons, tainted with excess and madness – which in turn relates to his incestuous devotion to his half-sister Augusta, and to the secret guilt of his typical heroes. The Prisoner's is a 'Byronic' consciousness without *guilt*, but obsessed with *race*. But while these points may explain how Byron was able to conceive the Prisoner, it does not follow that he approved of his causeless martyr.

Every poet invents what modern critics refer to as '*personae*'. If the poet writes a sonnet, he must adopt one of the voices formerly found for the sonnet form, or, with great difficulty, invent a new one. This difficulty arises because definitive works in the form, such as Petrarch's, Shakespeare's, or Wordsworth's, seem to have 'fused' particular intonations, particular rhetorical patterns, with the form itself. So Byron's sonnet on Chillon is, not surprisingly, voiced in the Miltonic tradition which Wordsworth had impressively revived, though he does not follow Milton's rhyme-scheme. It is a public sonnet, with a public, authoritative, voice.

The *persona* of the Prisoner is a Byronic invention. Byron fused metres adapted from Scott with a device as old in English as Chaucer's *Canterbury Tales*, whereby the voice of a poem is given to an invented or historical personage who is manifestly not the poet himself. Any individuality expressed through the verse is attributed to the *persona*, not to the poet.

A great successor of the Romantics, Yeats, called his personae 'masks' (this is in fact the English translation), and in his works, as scholars agree, the 'masks' take up antithetical positions. Yeats's mature vision of the world emerges not from 'straightforward'-looking statements 'in his own person', such as Wordsworth essayed so momentously when he wrote of the 'growth' of his own mind in *The Prelude*, but from the contradictory clash of his masks.

I think that Byron must be read as one reads Yeats, not as one reads Wordsworth. The *personae* of his verse, including the varied narrator-voices of his tales, are all to be taken *provisionally*. Byron is not, I believe, saying to himself, 'This is what I know or think or feel: how can I best communicate it?', but asking himself, 'What will happen if I make such-and-such a voice say this? What are the implications of this notion, this conception? What form might suit it, and how can I handle that form?' Wordsworth aspires to 'sincerity' and to 'authority'. Byron is always unsure as to what a 'sincere' utterance might sound like, and he assumes the authority of the confidence-trickster rather than that of the teacher.

He was precipitated in early youth from obscurity to a peerage, from the provincial Calvinism of Aberdeen to the lax Anglican milieu of Harrow School, where he consorted with young aristocrats. Unlike Wordsworth's, his mind didn't 'grow'. It was grafted.

# 3. 'Personality' and Convention: from *Childe Harold* to *Don Juan*

I have worked towards Byron's 'personality' from the outside – from the voices of his popular contemporaries, through the large historical phenomenon of Byronism, through the 'omniscient' narrative voice of *The Siege* and the obvious *persona* of *The Prisoner*, before confronting works which appear highly personal. I have what I think are strong reasons for doing this.

Byron's life is extremely fascinating, and no one need feel ashamed of finding it so. But we are concerned with him as a poet, not as a case-study in sexual deviance, or as a political activist. To have begun by discussing works which must be related to his singular life-history might have tempted us to indulge in the so-called 'biographical fallacy', seeking in details of the artist's life 'explanations' for everything in his work. It is a fallacy because the poet's struggle with his material, with words, with forms, is an experience in itself. However much he strives to draw on his own daily doings and spontaneous feelings, the form which he is using will dictate certain phrasings, rule out others – and suggest to him new states of feeling and new ideas which would not have surfaced without his technical struggle.

Furthermore, Byron's adult life was lived in a 'glare of publicity'. His best-selling verse tales were in a medium pioneered by others. Such personal feeling as he could express emerged partly in struggle against, but partly also in connivance with, the role accorded him by admirers and foes, and with styles handed on to him. There is a lot of posturing in Byron, a lot of playing up to his public image and to the requirements of the emergent 'Byronic' discourse. There are also debts to Scott and Thomas Moore and, behind these contemporaries, to Pope, Milton, Shakespeare, Dante.

Even among his numerous short poems, many are deliberately conventional exercises, sometimes brilliant, in modes developed by other writers. Skelton prints two famous poems published together in a collection called *Hebrew Melodies* (1815), which was prefaced by a note from the author:

> The subsequent poems were written at the request of my friend, the Hon. D. Kinnaird, for a Selection of Hebrew Melodies, and have been published, with the music, arranged by Mr Braham and Mr Nathan.

Please now read 'The Destruction of Sennacherib' (page 31), then 'She Walks in Beauty' (page 27). Is the first in any sense personal (or Byronic)? Is 'She Walks in Beauty' primarily erotic, or religious?

DISCUSSION

'Sennacherib' is a brilliant short narrative, in no real sense 'personal'. Byron's *persona* is a collective one: the Old Testament Jews rejoice over their fallen foe.

Had you perhaps imagined that Byron wrote 'She walks in beauty' to celebrate a woman whom he loved, or was aiming to seduce? Well, you weren't necessarily far wrong. Though it was published alongside works 'written to order', Byron seems to have been inspired to write it by the beauty of a cousin-by-marriage seen at a party in London, Anne Wilmot. Its publication in *Hebrew Melodies*, however, indicates that Byron felt he'd achieved more than a personal statement. The religious coloration of the language ('heaven', 'pure', 'goodness', 'innocent') is suited to a 'sacred' context, and, to make an all-too-obvious point, 'cloudless climes and starry skies' are more suggestive of Palestine than of London. But Byron was certainly not thinking of Palestine as he wrote it, since Kinnaird only suggested the *Melodies* project three months after the poem was drafted in June 1814. The Mediterranean lands which Byron had visited – Portugal, Spain, Albania, Greece, Turkey – would have suggested 'cloudless climes'. Meanwhile, his lovely (though third-person) compliment belonged to a recognizable genre. Byron's friend Thomas Moore had, since 1808, been publishing popular *Irish Melodies*, and could readily turn out a 'song' such as this:

Why does azure deck the sky?
  'Tis to be like thy looks of blue;
Why is red the rose's dye?
  Because it is thy blushes' hue.
All that's fair, by Love's decree.
Has been made resembling thee ...

or this 'Ode to Nea, written at Bermuda':

Behold the leafy mangrove, bending
  O'er the waters blue and bright,
Like Nea's silky lashes, lending
  Shadow to her eyes of light![1]

To quote Moore is to show how Byron transcends conventions which he, like Moore, had adapted from a tradition stretching back to the Elizabethans. It was far from original to compare a lovely woman with anything and everything deemed to be beautiful in nature, and richly traditional to associate outward beauty with inward virtue. I conjecture that we have in 'she walks in beauty' an excellent example of how the 'struggle' with language and form may produce a 'feeling' never before expressed. Byron's lyric exposes the crudity of Moore and of many others working in the tradition to which it belongs. The movement of the verse is slowed, the tone made reflective and tender, by his brilliant handling of the simple device of expanding a basic quatrain to a six-line stanza, repeating the same rhymes. Note the heavy punctuation (colon, semicolon) at the ends of lines 4 and 10. Strike out, mentally, the two final lines of each stanza. You will see how the remaining quatrains would have made by themselves, a pretty poem. But the additions (lines 5–6, lines 11–12) create the sense that the speaker's mind is in genuine awe of this loveliness, is searching behind sweet appearance for inner sweetness.

Not for Byron the banality of Moore's direct exotic comparison – 'beloved's eyelashes are like a mangrove tree'. The 'exotic' flavour is delicately conveyed by 'cloudless climes'. Byron concentrates not on the palpable beauty of the woman's exterior, but on her expression, her 'personality', defined in terms of light and dark and of a perfect, tremulous balance between them. She is not statically beautiful – she *walks* in beauty. I can remember no earlier lyric in the tradition which projects as strongly such a concept of admiring mind and allured senses, not only moved but tested by the woman who impresses them.

This very beautiful poem is not a 'portrait' of a relative seen among the Whig grandees at Lansdowne House, dressed 'in mourning, with dark spangles on her dress'.[2] As its place in *Hebrew*

*Melodies* implies, it projects a chaste awe of beauty such as we might imagine to have been felt by a Hebrew patriarch in the days of Abraham – and such as novelists since Byron, in parts thanks to him, have been able to award to their characters.

Could you please now read 'So, we'll go no more a roving' (Skelton, page 23).


DISCUSSION

Byron wrote a long letter to Thomas Moore, from Venice, dated 28 February 1817, in which he included the whole lyric.

> . . . Your last indicated that you were unwell. At present, I am on the invalid regimen myself. The Carnival – that is, the latter part of it – and sitting up late o'nights, had knocked me up a little. But it is over, – and it is now Lent, with all its abstinence and Sacred Music.
>
> The mumming closed with a masked ball at the Fenice, where I went, as also to most of the ridottos, etc., etc.,; and, though I did not dissipate much upon the whole, yet I find 'the sword wearing out the scabbard', though I have but just turned the corner of twenty-nine.

> So we'll go no more a roving
>   So late into the night,
> Though the heart be still as loving,
>   And the moon be still as bright . . . [etc.][3]

Read 'in context', the poem seems flip: 'I'm exhausted by a sexual and alcoholic orgy. No more adventures – for the time being.' But detached from the letter, the poem seems impersonal. Its opening line makes it clear that a folk song, 'The Jolly Beggar', was in Byron's mind:

> Nae mair I'll gang a-rovin
>   A-rovin in the nicht
> Nae mair I'll gang a-rovin
>   Though the meen shines e'er sae bricht.

(This is the chorus transcribed as sung by the great Jeannie Robertson, from Aberdeen, in our own day.[4]) The words 'no more' go beyond the direct projection of one person's temporary exhaustion. The poem could apply to two situations at least:

1 A love affair has ended – 'we'll go no more a roving, though our hearts are still as loving' (towards other lovers?) and the night is still 'made for loving' (others, physically). The partner addressed is like an outworn sheath, to be discarded.

2 The speaker has exhausted his emotional, perhaps even his physical, capacity for love. He confronts his own mortality. The spirit ('sword') outwears its body ('sheath').

Neither reading can exclude the other. Whatever its rather brutish genesis was, in a hung-over head where a folk-song phrase took lodging, the poem expresses a complex of feelings with compact subtlety. It contains no clear biographical reference whatsoever. The other person included in 'we' might be a woman, or a male friend, companion in adventure. We might think of a weary Don Giovanni addressing his servant, his Leporello. Or 'we' could be merely a poetical way of saying 'I'. Knowledge of Byron's life merely instructs us that any or all of these options may have occurred to him.

Let's now look at 'personal' poems by Byron in the context of his career, which can be divided into three phases:

(i) *Till 1812*: Byron was trying out two 'serious' voices. One, used in lyrical and reflective pieces, was 'Romantic' much in the manner of Scott and Moore. The other, at odds with the first, was worked up in his verse satire *English Bards and Scotch Reviewers* and derived from his eighteenth-century predecessors in the heroic couplet, Pope and Charles Churchill (1731–64).

(ii) *1812–17*: From the publication of the first part of *Childe Harold's Pilgrimage* till his short verse narrative *Beppo*, Byron was mostly engulfed in 'Byronism'.

(iii) *1817–24*: Having discovered, with *Beppo*, a stanza-form in which he could relax, Byron undermined 'Byronism' in his immense *Don Juan*, while exploring it further in the 'objective' medium of drama. (Following his start with *Manfred* (1816), he wrote several plays. They were for the reader, not for the theatre, but they are not without dramatic vigour.) His last short narrative, *The Island*, very interestingly, mixes 'Byronic' passages with others in his new *Juan* manner.

Through all three phases, Byron indulged his gift for 'occasional' light verse. By the time he began *Juan* he was practised in a wide variety of styles, and could produce them at will.

Could you please now read 'To the Author of a Sonnet' (Skelton, page 18), 'Written after Swimming' (page 20) and 'To Thomas Moore' (page 22). How would you 'characterize' the tone of these verses and the personality which they project?

DISCUSSION

Though these poems span all three phases of Byron's career, I think you'll agree that they share a common 'personality'. They are playful, buoyant, and unlaboured – as far from the measured satire of Pope as from the lyrical voice of Wordsworth.

Now please consider 'Remember thee!' (Skelton, page 20), 'The spell is broke' (page 21) and 'Lines on Hearing that Lady Byron was Ill' (page 41). Does the 'voice' seem consistent with those of the poems we've just looked at?

## DISCUSSION

Surely the answer is 'yes'. The indignation of 'Remember thee!' is tempered by wit: the balance of the last line makes the whole curse seem elegant, detached. 'The spell is broke' reads like a clever *jeu d'esprit*. The 'Lines' to his wife are of course more complex – amongst the most 'personal' which he ever wrote. But as with 'Remember thee!', we feel, don't we, something akin to playfulness? The heavy sarcasm of the opening, the disgusted hauteur of the close, such a brilliant but hyperbolic phrase as 'moral Clytemnestra', suggest that Byron is *dramatizing* his feelings, 'piling it on' for effect.

Now please read 'One struggle more' (Skelton, page 29), 'And thou art dead' (page 34) and 'If sometimes' (page 37). Again, is there any consistency?

## DISCUSSION

These resulted from Byron's love for a Cambridge choirboy, John Edleston, with whom he fell in love when an undergraduate, and whose death in 1811 moved him deeply. Their relationship was complicated by difference of social class, and perhaps by Byron's inability to come to terms with his own bisexuality. Direct expression of his love for Edleston would have been extremely dangerous. Louis Crompton's recent study of *Byron and Greek Love* (1985) emphasises the extent of 'homophobia' in Regency Britain. Hostility towards male homosexuals had been mounting, and the 'decades of greatest animosity coincided almost exactly with Byron's lifetime'. The Evangelical-Christian 'Society for the Suppression of Vice' founded by William Wilberforce in 1788, the year of the poet's birth, 'set the tone for the new century' and strongly influenced the administration of justice. Public executions for 'buggery' averaged two a year. Other homosexuals suffered the danger and public humiliation of being placed in the pillory and pelted by the mob with dead cats and blood from the butchers, with rotten eggs and dung. Ironically, when Lord Castlereagh and Foreign Secretary committed suicide, Byron, who detested his politics, could not restrain from jibing, in his preface to Cantos VI–

VIII of *Don Juan*, at his homosexual proclivities, rumours about which had had a part in his decision to kill himself.[5]

But Byron's own decision to live abroad can be related to the greater tolerance of homosexuality shown in Europe, where there were no executions for the 'crime' after the French Revolution. While his heterosexual impulses were strong and persistent, he did display his homosexual leanings very strongly in the period from his Harrow schooldays to his exile in Italy. They returned in his last days as a freedom fighter in Greece. There is no doubt that powerful feeling inspired the three poems which we are inspecting. Yet they are surely more 'conventional' than 'She Walks in Beauty'. Their sentiments could have been expressed by any gifted writer within European tradition. Though touching and elegant, they lack strong individuality.

Finally, look at 'Stanzas to Augusta' (page 43).


DISCUSSION

Of all the women in his life, Byron cared longest and probably deepest for his half-sister Augusta Leigh. She shared his 'lineage', he felt secure with his own Byronic 'race', she was, besides, a good-natured young woman. But these well-known stanzas are strongly 'Byronic'. The poem could perfectly well have been called 'Conrad to Medora' and included in The *Corsair*.

The Byronic voice of Byron had its most lengthy expression in *Childe Harold*. This poem, which made Byron a 'star', is unique in English literature. He worked on it over several years. He began it during his Mediterranean travels in 1809–11. The first two cantos were published by John Murray in 1812, and caused a sensation. People wept at public readings. Illustrations showed Harold looking much like Byron, at whose feet society women threw themselves. Scandal led to his exile. Abroad again, he resumed work on it. Canto 3 appeared in 1816, Canto 4 in 1818.

In McGann's edition of Byron's poems, *Childe Harold* occupies the whole of volume 2, 180 pages of verse, plus 78 pages of topographical, ethnographical and historical notes by Byron and his friend Hobhouse. The many avid purchasers of Cantos 1 and 2 received for their money, besides other long notes, a 33-page disquisition on the Romaic language (modern Greek) with a facsimile folding plate of Romaic calligraphy.

'Childe' is a medieval word for 'Knight', so we should expect a chivalric tone and subject-matter. 'Harold' was the name of the last

King of Saxon England, and so suggests both Englishness and
doom. 'Pilgrimage' evokes medieval Catholicism. Byron's title
bestows on his poem an air of archaism and mystery. Both are
enhanced by his choice of metre. The stanza employed by the
Elizabethan poet Edmund Spenser in his *Faerie Queene* had been
revived by James Thomson in the mid-eighteenth century. Spenser's
verse appealed greatly to Romantic taste, but Byron does not seem
to have cared for it particularly. (He did not read Spenser until he
had finished most of *Harold*, and modelled his handling of the
stanza on James Beattie's *The Minstrel* of 1771.) He said that he
chose it because its use was associated with tonal and structural
flexibility. He could mix tones and moods and wander freely from
topic to topic.

Harold inaugurates 'Byronism' – he is a great sinner who
'lov'd but one,/And that lov'd one, alas! could ne'er be his.' Sated
with pleasure, he leaves his ancestral hall in Britain and, saying
goodbye to no one, travels in Europe, brooding. Indifferent to both
nature and humanity, he is merely a gloomy lay figure to set in this
scene or that.

Canto 1 takes us to Iberia, where the Peninsular War, England
and Spain *versus* France, is currently raging. There is an exciting
set-piece description of a bullfight. In Canto 2 Harold travels to
Greece. Or rather, the narrator travels to Greece, meditates on its
ancient ruins, denounces Lord Elgin for taking those famous
marbles from the Parthenon to Britain – and then suddenly exclaims,
after fifteen stanzas:

> But where is Harold? shall I then forget
> To urge the gloomy wanderer o'er the wave?

A description of a voyage from Spain to Albania follows, then a
land travelogue, then further meditations on the sad servitude of
modern Greece. In short, the poem follows Byron's itinerary of
1809–11 and embodies his reflections on his travels. The archaism
and romance implied by title and by stanza-form were denied to
Byron's readers – who, bewitched by his rhetoric, didn't object!

By the time Canto 3 was published, late in 1816, 'Byronism'
was an established cultural fact. The narrator resumes his task as a
full-fledged Byronist in his own right:

>         . . . I *have* thought
> Too long and darkly, till my brain became,
> In its own eddy boiling and o'erwrought,
> A whirling gulf of phantasy and flame:
> And thus, untaught in youth my heart to tame,
> My springs of life were poison'd . . .

Harold, meanwhile, has changed. He has learnt to accept Despair. He has become a Rousseauist, a Wordsworthian even, a lover of nature. Unable to 'herd with Man', he seeks wild places:

> The desert, forest, cavern, breaker's foam,
> Were unto him companionship . . .

Following Byron's own itinerary of 1816, he proceeds first to the field of Waterloo, then up the historic valley of the Rhine to Switzerland – to the Alps, to the haunts of Rousseau.

In his dedication to Canto 4, Byron admits that 'there will be found less of the pilgrim than in any of the preceding, and that little slightly, if at all, separated from the author speaking in his own person. The fact is, that I had become weary of drawing a line which every one seemed determined not to perceive.' The mask is dropped, Byron and Harold are one, and Canto 4 can be read only as a sustained, personal meditation upon Italy, where Byron had settled. From Venice we move south to Rome – 'lone mother of dead empires' – where gigantic ruins dwarf the 'petty misery' of Byronism. Napoleon takes his place in a meditation on history, a 'vain man', 'coquettish in ambition'.

Please now turn again to the extracts from Canto 4 which I asked you to include in your preliminary reading (pages 49–58– stanzas XCIII–XCVIII; (CXXII–CXXXV; and CLXXVII–CLXXXVI.)

As you read, please consider your reactions

1 to Byron's handling of his chosen stanza form;
2 to his diction (ornate or plain?);
3 to his 'philosophizing' – what sort of world-view is being expressed? and
4 to any shifts of tone (of 'voice') which you detect.

DISCUSSION

Byron handles the old Spenserian stanza with astonishing new skill and energy. He exploits the fact that the dawdling, slackening, final alexandrine checks the movement of the preceding lines. The 'fall' of the stanza may match the fall of human hopes, the trailing away of the speaker's energetic, indignant voice, into resignation, if not despair. Or the greater length of the last line, its weightiness, may be used to 'clinch', reinforce what has been proposed, as in stanza XCVIII.

The diction is 'traditional', varied yet restrained. It can admit such a resounding Latinism as 'Opinion and omnipotence', but is on the whole plain – the last line of XCIII consists, you will notice, of twelve monosyllables, and every word in it belongs to basic English vocabulary. There is neither archaism (such as Byron, parodically, had played with in Canto 1) nor topical slanginess and exuberant word-play (such as he would employ in *Don Juan*). The rhetoric is highly wrought but not pretentious; the voice is authoritative because it stands four-square in English tradition.

And in great part its burden is traditional. Vanity, says the preacher – all is vanity. There are ample Biblical, medieval, Renaissance precedents for questioning the significance of human action, and for stressing cyclical, repetitive patterns in history. But from general reflections which would not have surprised the author of Ecclesiastes, we move to very specific reflections on contemporary Europe. What is the 'freedom' which the speaker extols, its banner, in a most memorable, if odd, image, streaming 'like the thunder-storm *against* the wind'? Its content is defined by negatives. It eschews slavery and 'chains'. It is not Tyranny, and Ambition thwarts it. And its enemies are clearly identified in the political context of 1818 from which Byron writes. Europe's current rulers 'ape' Napoleon (stanza XCV). The terror of 1793, the rise of Napoleon, which followed it, and the 'base pageant' of Napoleonic return from exile to final defeat, are used by them as 'pretext' for maintaining the thraldom which, the speaker implies, had been the common lot of men down the ages.

The greatest achievement of this rhetoric is that it sets the day-to-day politics of the moment in the context of all historical time, all geographical space. Those who fight for freedom stand opposed to nothing less than an 'eternal thrall', but their cause is symbolized by the recuperative power of nature, which burgeons every spring. A voice replete with authority gives its readers of 1818 a cosmological/historical framework in which a blow for freedom would make sense, despite the risks, of failure and corruption, that the same voice fully acknowledges. The alternatives to resistance are thralldom – and despair. But the speaker has to acknowledge the claims of despair.

In stanza CXXI, not printed by Skelton, Byron avers that love is a human creation:

> Oh Love! no habitant of earth thou art –
> An unseen seraph, we believe in thee.
> A faith whose martyrs are the broken heart,
> But never yet hath seen, nor e'er shall see
> The naked eye, thy form, as it should be;
> The mind hath made thee, as it peopled heaven.
> Even with its own desiring phantasy,
> And to a thought such shape and image given.
> As haunts the unquench'd soul – parch'd – wearied – wrung – and
>    riven.

We would be happier, Byron suggests in CXXII, if we could not invent Love, Beauty and other ideals. Man, not God, creates perfect forms, Man creates 'The unreach'd Paradise of our despair'. Vanity, vanity, the voice insists; the old theme is varied with freshness and skill. Stanza CXXVI is as compact an expression as one could find of Byron's Calvinism-without-God. The whole world is to us a upas tree (this East Indian plant was alleged to be so poisonous that it killed all animal life for fifteen miles around it), because man is inherently sinful, at odds with the 'harmony of things', with nature outside him. But from sin there is no salvation – our souls are 'immedicable', there is no cure.

*Homo Byronicus*, however, is defiant. Thought is perhaps the cause of all his woes (if we were like birds, or stones, we would not be unhappy). But it is our right, it gives us a refuge – in self-respect. By an effort of stubborn will, Byron's speaker identifies himself with the cause of Reason, with the belief of the 'Enlightened' men of the eighteenth century, that to know the truth is a good in itself from which other goods may follow. Reason is the *divine* faculty, it is what is God-like in man.

Had Skelton ended his excerpt at CXXIX, we would have had an impressive, free-standing expression of Byron's cosmological-historical vision. But what he further provides is a shift typical of the poem's transitions from voice to voice, from stance to stance. The speaker descends to personality. He dramatizes himself, his sufferings, his 'ancestral' taint ('lineage' again). He boasts (CXXXIV); and this makes him seem uncertain of himself. He claims the power to make successful curses – then mitigates this absurdity with a simple histrionic effect (CXXXV): 'You thought I meant that, didn't you, reader? But really I forgive them all. And don't think I do so from Christian charity. It's just that I'm so much superior to *those* wretches. Had to be, you see – couldn't have survived otherwise.' I offer a comic 'translation', which may seem inappropriate. But in fact Byron is not far from the manner of *Don Juan*, which will permit a swift transition from invective to humour and even to self-mockery.

The celebrated apostrophe to the Ocean which concludes *Childe Harold* appears at first glance to evince a Wordsworthian awe of Nature and of the Almighty. Not at second. Its main thrust is social, being anti-social. The sea is applauded for what it is not, and for what it wrecks and drowns. It is an element indifferent to man, but the speaker of the poem does not fear it. Even as a child he could put his hand on its 'mane'; the lion which frightened others had no terror for him. *Harold* ends with a prodigious assertion of its speaker's superiority to the rest of the human race, even to the empires of 'Assyria, Greece, Rome, Carthage'. How did this passage impress you?


DISCUSSION

To me it seems flatulent. The imagery is fluent but careless, such as a gifted writer in full stride might well produce as he hurried to finish a book for publication. 'Thy fields/Are not a spoil for him' is manifestly untrue: Byron ignores the importance of sea-fishing in human economy. Having fused the sea with the Almighty, 'eternity' and the Invisible, the speaker produces a rather delicious inadvertent bathos, alluding to its slime and its sea-monsters. He has yet to make the transition from Byronism (which takes itself seriously, and is undermined by bathos) to Juanism. The term 'Juanism' can be applied not only to *Don Juan* itself but to two shorter, though not short, narratives: *Beppo* (1817) and *The Vision of Judgement* (1822) – other products of Byron's 'third phase' (see p. 41).

Juanism takes to the limit the implications of Byronism's prior discovery that all is vanity in a godless universe. It *enthrones* bathos alongside reason. It does not forget the Bible, Milton, Dante, Pope, but it draws from the wise masters of Enlightened prose – Fielding and Sterne, Voltaire and Gibbon – and also from the spirit of opera, which had reached its comic summit in Mozart's *Don Giovanni* and *Così fan tutte* (1787, 1790) and was being carried forward in Byron's chosen homeland, Italy, by Gioacchino Rossini and his rivals.

Stendhal, the French novelist, wrote of Rossini in 1824:

> Napoleon is dead; but a new conqueror has already shown himself to the world; and from Moscow to Naples, from London to Vienna, from Paris to Calcutta, his name is constantly on every tongue.[6]

His name was certainly on Byron's tongue. The poet Leigh Hunt stayed with him in 1822 and recalled:

> Lord Byron, who used to sit up at night, writing Don Juan (which he did under the influence of gin and water), rose late in the morning. He breakfasted; read; lounged about, singing an air, generally out of Rossini, and in a swaggering style, though in a voice at once small and veiled; then took a bath, and was dressed; and coming downstairs, was heard, still singing, in the courtyard . . .[7]

In Italy, where Byron attended opera as a matter of course, there was no reverential silence as passions were howled and trilled, no separation of 'culture' from life. I think it is helpful to see *Don Juan* in the context of *opera buffa*, a medium for Mozart and Rossini –

of a highly artificial form, which was nevertheless 'open' to everyday experience, which was supremely histrionic, yet also suffused with the pathos, and farce, and fitful dignity, of human nature. Its presence seems as obvious to me in Byron's poem as in Stendhal's fiction. Thomas Babington Macaulay, in 1831, sneered that its 'first and best cantos' were but 'a feeble copy of the Page in the Marriage of Figaro'.

Before we turn to *Juan* at last, please re-read *The Vision of Judgement*. It makes sense to discuss this shorter 'Juanist' narrative first.

# 4.  *The Vision of Judgement*

*The Vision of Judgement* has to be understood in the context of Byron's politics, which were both libertarian and 'aristocratical'. Bertrand Russell, himself an aristocrat and a kind of rebel, wrote of Byron:

> It is obvious that an aristocrat does not become a rebel unless his temperament and circumstances are in some way peculiar. Byron's circumstances were very peculiar. His earlier recollections were of his parents' quarrels; his mother was a woman whom he feared for her cruelty and despised for her vulgarity; his nurse combined wickedness with the strictest Calvinist theology; his lameness filled him with shame, and prevented him from being one of the herd at school. At ten years old, after living in poverty, he suddenly found himself a Lord and the owner of Newstead.[1]

Byron's mother, if not such a monster as Russell implies, was a highly emotional woman who had suffered a great deal. She came from the great Highland family of Gordon, prominent throughout Scottish history from the early middle ages, and much sung in folklore for the violent exploits of its members. While the Byrons had been Royalists in the Civil Wars, the Gordons had remained identified with Catholicism after the Reformation. Byron's respect for his ancestors was liable to pull him towards conservative values.

On the other hand, his Aberdeen upbringing had brough him into much closer contact with ordinary people than most English peers had ever enjoyed. His most thorough biographer has concluded that 'the whole environment of Byron's Aberdeen years conditioned him to the views of the lower-middle class Scottish world with which he was daily associated in the streets and later at school . . . [where he] mingled freely with his classmates on a plane of equality'.[2] His mother, though fiercely proud of her Gordon forebears, sympathized with the people's cause in the French Revolution.

In 1812 Byron made an oration in the House of Lords which set him on the 'extreme left' of the Whigs. Lower-class 'Luddites' had reacted to bad times in the Midlands textile industry by breaking machines. Byron spoke up for these 'honest and indus- trious' people. E. P. Thompson, in his *Making of the English Working Class*, links him with other 'radicals' of the period:

> If we are to understand the extremism of Burdett and Cochrane in 1810, we need only read Byron. Such men despised the scramble for power and riches, the hypocrisy of their own class and the pretensions of the new rich. In their frustration they dreamed perhaps at times of some revolutionary spasm which would overthrow the whole fabric of 'Old Corruption'.

Thompson's last suggestion is verified by Byron's letter to Tom Moore of Christmas Eve, 1816, in which he includes a 'Luddite' song by himself. Byron, in Venice, asks Moore, in England, jocularly: 'Are you not near the Luddites? By the Lord! if there's a row, but I'll be among ye! How go on the weavers – the breakers of frames – the Lutherans of politics – the reformers?'[4] Byron – 'joking apart' – did have occasional visions of flinging himself to the head of a revolution in England.

But when his close friend Hobhouse stood as a radical candidate for the Westminster constituency, Byron wrote to his publisher Murray (February 1820) that he was worried about the low-class company which Hobhouse was keeping: 'a pack of blackguards – who disgust one with their Cause – although I have always been a friend to and a Voter for reform . . . If we must have a tyrant – let him at least be a gentleman who has been bred to the business, and let us fall by the axe and not by the butcher's cleaver . . . .'[5]

Byron's respect for the Irish Whig, Henry Grattan, was significant. His interest in Irish grievances probably stemmed from his friendship for Moore, who voiced Irish patriotism genteelly in song, but never with such violence as to get himself debarred from polite society. In 1782 the Irish Protestant land-owning and middle classes led by Grattan had won independence for their Dublin Parliament within the British Empire. In 1798 a widely supported insurrection was put down with much blood. Two years later the Dublin Parliament disappeared in a Union with Britain. Byron's frequent expressions of outrage over the oppression of Ireland can be set beside his active support for Italy's liberation from Austrian rule and for Greek freedom from Turkish despotism. He was all in favour of nationalist revolutions, under aristocratic leadership, in foreign countries. He was not so attracted by insurrection in England, where he had property and a title. However, his friendship with Shelley, and his close relations with Leigh Hunt, ensured his continued involvement with British radicalism – as did frequent attacks on him by the Tory press in Britain, and a vengeful assault by Robert Southey.

Robert Southey, with Wordsworth and Coleridge, made up the so-called 'Lake School' of poets. The Tory Establishment had created Southey Poet Laureate in 1813. He wrote vast amounts of polished non-fictional prose, but it is now unread, like almost all his verse, except by scholars. Southey was a model of domestic propriety, Christian rectitude, and Tory orthodoxy. Marilyn Butler tells us:

> With the restoration of peace, the stage was set for literary war . . . Between 1814 and 1819 the major poets and novelists virtually all made some kind of appearance on the public stage, often to comment on the political implications of the work of other writers.

Wordsworth's new long poem, *The Excursion* distressed younger poets who had learnt from him. In it

> they found a poem . . . which aspires to permanence in a traditional, institutional, orthodox Christian vein. Wordsworth celebrates the victory against innovatory, Voltairean France, but he claims that it will be final only if England holds to her inner strength – if Englishmen are pious, dutiful and inwardly secure. . . .

(She adds 'In the long run the classic riposte to *The Excursion* was Byron's *Don Juan*, which gaily substituted a sexual ethic for Wordsworth's solemn asceticism.[6]) While Coleridge preached *Lay*

*Sermons* advocating traditional values, his brother-in-law Southey also wrote on public issues, and, like him, supported press censorship. In his republican youth (1794) Southey had penned a revolutionary play, *Wat Tyler*. A left-wing printer, Sherwin, got hold of a copy and gleefully published it in 1817. Southey sought an injunction against him for infringement of copyright, but the ultra-Tory judge Lord Eldon refused it on the grounds that the Court 'could not take notice of property in the unhallowed profits of libellous publications'. To complete the Laureate's discomfiture, the pirated books made large profits, and so subsidized less lucrative ventures by the same radical press against which Southey himself inveighed.[7]

So Byron found Southey a ready-made target – he was, in fact, a latecomer to a long-standing affray. As he worked on the first Canto of *Don Juan* in 1818, he heard that Southey had been spreading a rumour that Byron and Shelley had formed a 'League of Incest' to fornicate mutually with two sisters. 'He lied like a rascal, for they *were not Sisters*'.[8] Claire Clairmont, mother of Byron's daughter Allegra, was not sister to Shelley's wife Mary – she was daughter of Mary's stepmother by a former husband. In any case, Byron never had intercourse with Mary, though Shelley probably did so with Claire. Outraged, Byron wrote the 'Dedication' to *Don Juan* which you will find on pp. 135 ff.

Byron left this out of the first instalment of *Don Juan*, published in 1819, on the advice of his publisher and friends, who feared that the reading public would find it offensive. (One particular point to which they objected was Byron's use of the current slang term, 'dry bob', meaning 'coition without [male] emission'.) The 'Dedication' was not printed with *Juan* till 1833. Will you now please re-read it? What is Byron's *main* target?

DISCUSSION

Not really Southey *in particular*? The 'Dedication' is one of the most exhilarating pieces of invective in English, but, in view of Byron's personal reasons for anger against Southey, its most remarkable trait is its good humour. The 'Lake Poets' are attacked not only for their Toryism, but for their egotism. Southey wants to 'be the only Blackbird in the dish'. He, Wordsworth and Coleridge believe that 'Poesy has wreaths' only for them. Byron himself will not be so vain and ungenerous. It's true that they've 'coined their self-love' (line 42), and so Byron can brand them with one of his finest lines, which may be unpacked like this: 'Self-love nowadays has cash value; the idea that the poet is an exceptional, isolated individual suits the Establishment very well; even so, the Lakers *debase* their own self-love, as Kings have "debased" coinage, by turning it into the petty vice of vanity – they get titles (Poet Laureate) as well as salaries'. But Byron concedes them to be 'poets still', with a due place on Parnassus.

Southey is small fry, after all. Byron reserves his bitterest words for Lord Castlereagh, the Foreign Secretary (1812–22), and these are extraordinarily savage. To the main cause of affront – that Castlereagh's policy, as at the Congress of Vienna, 1814–15, is designed to shore up and protect reactionary monarchies all over Europe – is added his former complicity, as secretary to the Lord Lieutenant in Dublin, in the bloody suppression of the 1798 rebellion, and his subsequent 'treacherous' role (he was himself Irish) in arranging the Union of 1800. After a violent yet measured onslaught on Castlereagh, Byron returns to Southey only to tease him. *Granted* that the Government's cause is an atrocious one – Southey can't even write in its favour effectively (line 128).

Southey never read this prodigious put-down. But he heard of it and wrote to a friend, 'Attack me as he will, I shall not go out of my course to break a spear with him; but if it comes in my way to give him a passing touch, it will be one that will leave a scar' (to C. H. Townsend, 20 July 1819).[9]

Only old men then had the dimmest memory of days when England had not been under the nominal rule of George III. He had assended his throne in 1760, and in his early days as ruler had faced cries from the Whig politicians he ousted that his evil advisers were aiming to restore monarchical despotism. An opportunist, John Wilkes, roused huge mobs and the slogan, 'Wilkes and Liberty'; this was heard in the then American colonies, inflamed feeling there, and helped to generate the American Revolution. Later, George had relapsed into innocent illness, suffering from a disease which produced the symptoms of madness. His feebleness had helped to confirm Parliament as the effectual sovereign of the British Empire, and there was, by 1820, no cause for a libertarian to detest him; fury could be reserved for 'his' Cabinet.

Laureate Southey now had to fulfil his official duties. A short formal ode might have satisfied the conscience of a man less vain about his office. Southey, however, projected a long poem portraying the King's entry into heaven. Furthermore, he pervesely chose to experiment with a metre little used in English for the very good reason that it didn't suit the language – namely the classical hexameter. Though Southey, in his time, had produced some agreeable light verse, his sense of humour was not capacious. We are indebted to him for *Botany Bay Eclogues* which include the *deathless lines:*

> Alone is heard the kangaroo's sad note
> Deepening in distance. Welcome, wilderness. . . .[10]

His *Vision of Judgement* begins

> 1. The Trance
> 'Twas at that sober hour when the light of day
>     is receding,
> And from surrounding things the hue wherewith
>     day has adorn'd them
> Fade, like the hopes of youth . . .(I)

Footnote 1 reads:

> This effect of twilight, and in the very scene described, has been lately represented by Mr. William Westall, in one of his Views of the Lakes, with the true feeling and power of genius. The range of mountains which is described in these introductory lines, may also be seen in his View of the Vale of Keswick from the Penrith road.

At his home in the Lake District, in a trance, occasioned by the beauty of the evening and religious thoughts upon George III's death, Southey is promised by an awesome Voice that the secrets of the Grave shall be revealed to him. He duly beholds the King, rising from the dead, and at once, no longer deranged, enquiring anxiously after the 'weal of his country'. George is reassured that Britain is doing very nicely, thank you. Napoleon has been defeated. Unfortunately, though, the 'Souls of the Wicked' and the 'Powers of Evil' are at work spreading revolutionary ideas among the masses.

Despite this disturbing news, the King proceeds to the Gate of Heaven:

> O'er the adamantine gates an Angel stood on the summit.
> Ho! he exclaimed, King George of England cometh to judgement!
> Hear Heaven! Ye Angels hear! Souls of the good and the Wicked
> Whom it concerns, attend!

The heavenly multitudes flock around, as do the Souls of the (revolutionary) Wicked. A hideous Demon arrives, with many heads and many voices:

> And in the hubbub of senseless sounds the watchwords of faction,
> Freedom, Invaded Rights, Corruption, and War, and Oppression
> Loudly enounced were heard . . .

(Note that Southey thinks that Freedom is a naughty word and that it is wrong to stir up resistance to Corruption, to War and to Oppression.) The Demon produces as accusers John Wilkes and the anonymous Junius, author of famous opposition pamphlets. But they are too abashed by their exalted surroundings to speak, so the irate Demon slings them back into hell and quickly departs himself.

Now the Soul of George Washington stands forth to absolve George III. Washington is not yet completely purified by heaven, but he sturdily acknowledges that the King acted, in that little matter of the American Revolution, 'with upright heart, as befitted a Sovereign.' This witness alone is enough, it seems, to secure the King entry to heaven. He drinks at the Well of Life, puts off his mortality, is rejuvenated, and passes, glorified, towards the Everlasting Portals to join Charles I, Elizabeth I, the Black Prince, Richard Coeur-de-Lion, Alfred the Great, and other English monarchs well known for their saintly behaviour. The *Quartier Anglais* of Heaven has been forwarned, and a crowd of British Worthies come out to meet him, Chaucer, Shakespeare, Spenser, Milton, along with Cranmer, martyr of Anglicanism, and the great soldier Duke of Marlborough. These stand by as George III's own dead heroic subjects rally to welcome him – Wolfe, Cook, Handel, Hogarth, Wesley ('whose zeal apostolic/though with error alloy'd, hath on earth its merited honour') etc. etc. – the climax arriving with Nelson's appearance. Southey, scrupulously exhaustive, does not omit Humphrey Davy, inventor of the Safety Lamp and a certain minor poet recently dead in his youth; both, as it happened, had been friends of the author.

At last George meets his entire family (such as have predeceased him). As the vast procession of virtuous English persons (a couple of Scots only are mentioned among them) passes through the everlasting Gates, Southey tries to push in with them.

> But the weight of the body withheld me. I stooped to the fountain,
> Eager to drink thereof, and to put away all that was earthly.
> Darkness came over me then at the chilling touch of the water,
> And my feet methought sunk, and I fell precipitate. Starting
> Then I awoke. . . .[11]

This preposterous effusion could safely have been left to gather the ridicule which it courted, and no doubt Byron would so have left it, had Southey not included, in his preface, several paragraphs denouncing 'lascivious' poets:

> ... Men of diseased hearts and depraved imaginations, who, forming a system of opinions to suit their own unhappy course of conduct, have rebelled against the holiest ordinances of human society, and hating that revealed religion which, with all their efforts and bravadoes, they are unable entirely to disbelieve, labour to make others as miserable as themselves, by infecting them with a moral virus that eats into the soul! The school which they have set up may properly be called the Satanic school ...
>
> This evil is political as well as moral, for indeed moral and political evils are inseparably connected ... Let rulers of the state look to this in time![12]

This gratuitous attack, with its final, hardly veiled, plea for censorship, was aimed directly at Byron and his *Don Juan*.

Byron's *Vision* appeared in the first issue of the *Liberal*. This was a journal which Byron had planned in Italy with Shelley and with Leigh Hunt, leader of the 'Cockney School' of poetry and friend of Keats, who stayed with Byron in Italy, sponged on him and rather annoyed him. Byron funded the journal.

I'm assuming that you read *The Vision* as part of your preliminary survey of Byron's verse. Before we look at it in detail, I'd like to turn to two of the most interesting questions about Byron's poetry that have been raised by critics. T. S. Eliot, in an elegant essay published in 1937, suggested that Byron should be viewed as a Scottish poet. As evidence for this unorthodox view, he instanced 'his peculiar diabolism, his delight in posing as a damned creature ... [which] could come only from the religious background of a people steeped in Calvinistic theology'. Eliot went on to argue that Byron's use of language was un-English. 'I cannot think of any other poet of his distinction who might so easily have been an accomplished foreigner writing English.' Byron, he argued, had to use a great many words to make his effects – he could not produce compact richness to match writers native to the tradition. *Don Juan*, Eliot contends, is Byron's greatest work, because he borrows an 'easy-going' stanza from the Italian which enables him to improvise at low intensity, expressing his personality freely. When, in the last four cantos of *Juan*, Byron takes his anti-hero to England, he produces something for which Eliot 'can find no parallel in English literature ... What Byron understands and dislikes about English society is very much what an intelligent foreigner ... would understand and dislike.' Finally, for his knock-out punch, Eliot produces a learned argument. Medieval Scottish poets had abused each other in long 'flytings' ('scolding-matches'). Praising the assault on Southey in Byron's dedication to *Juan*, Eliot contends that

This is not the satire of Dryden, still less of Pope ... This is not
indeed English satire at all; it is really a *flyting*, and closer in feeling
and intention to the satire of Dunbar:

Lene larbar, loungeour, baith lowsy in lisk and loyne;
Fy! skolderit skyn, thou art both skyre and strumple ...[13]

(These lines from William Dunbar's 'Flyting of Dunbar and
Kennedie' may be translated, 'Lean, impotent weakling, lounger,
lousy in both groin and loin; Fie! scorched skin, you are both
scratched and wrinkled ...')

The evidence for Byron's un-Englishness is very strong. Of all
British contemporaries, Scott was the one whom he most deeply
respected, and in his latter years reading and re-reading the
'Waverley' novels about Scottish history was a favourite pursuit. In
*Don Juan*, Canto 10, stanzas XVII–XVIII he wrote:

... but I am half a Scot by birth, and bred
A whole one, and my heart flies to my head,

As Auld Lang Syne brings Scotland, one and all,
    Scotch plaids, Scotch snoods, the blue hills, and clear streams,
The Dee, the Don, Balgounie's Brig's blackwall,
    All my boy feelings, all my gentler dreams
Of what I then dreamt, clothed in their own pall,
    Like Banquo's offspring. Floating past me seems
My childhood in this childishness of mine;
I care not – 'tis a glimpse of Auld Lang Syne.[14]

The language which a child learns from his mother, his nurse and
his school-fellows must remain that in which he feels most at ease.
Eliot's argument, therefore, is plausible. Yet Wordsworth, growing
up in northern England, and even Keats, a 'Cockney', were in a
position much like Byron's, as have been countless others before and
after them. The language of most poetry, a learned mode of
Standard English, is as alien to a Liverpudlian as to an Aberdonian.
Byron, with his expensive classical education at Harrow and
Cambridge, was actually better equipped than most to use it. Eliot's
case is fully persuasive only if we see Byron as *conscious* of the
artificiality, for him, of English as a medium, and as *aware* of the
alternative possibility of using his mother tongue, Scots.

He hadn't read Dunbar, so far as I know, or the 'flyting'
personal attacks which old Scottish poets had made on each other
with gusto. Such Scottish verse as there was between Dunbar (who
died in the early sixteenth century) and Burns (born in the mid-to-
late eighteenth) was not much, if at all, read or discussed in Byron's
circles. But in such circles every cultivated person knew Burns, and

Scott's collection of *Minstrelsy of the Scottish Border* (1802–03) had made Scottish folk song common literary currency. I think that Byron's relationship to Scottish tradition is extremely significant.[16] What Burns, and folk song, showed was that the language of everyday speech – Scots vernacular, or English slang – could be made into moving or very funny verse: that there need be no gulf such as even Wordsworth left between the public house and Parnassus.

The important issue here is not to decide whether Byron was 'Scottish' or 'English' – a sensible compromise would be to say that like Scott he was a Scottish-bred poet using the English language – but to clarify Byron's relationship with diction and form. Eliot is not the only critic to have seen something unusual in that relationship. Paul West offers a psychological, rather than cultural, diagnosis:

> Reduce everything he ever wrote, and you will find an essential act of repulsion: either self-emptying into a *persona*, or a repudiation. He pushes away what he is; he repudiates even the *persona* of Don Juan. He has the insecure person's fierce need of admiration; he needs to feel unobliged to his subject-matter, his friends, his publisher, his mistresses, his house, his rôle, his reputation. And yet . . . he seeks to eliminate this lust for elimination; and so he lands up with inappropriate impedimenta – the wrong woman, the wrong type of poem, the wrong reputation, the wrong stanza form, and so on.[17]

We can combine cultural and psychological explanations. Byron, an Aberdeen boy sent to Harrow, *was* 'insecure', in his relationship with the upper-class English culture which he met there. Did he feel a fraud acting out his part as English lord? His castigation of 'society' was fuelled by the genuine contempt of an outsider who had seen high life from the inside, knew it well, but hadn't been reared to it. He often wrote, in letters, about his verse as something he hoped to grow out of. Not for him Wordsworth's complete certainty. *Childe Harold*, as we have seen, was, in its flouting of readers' expectations, a vast piece of impudence. He got away with it, but he could not feel 'inward' with the language he used, even though others admired his use of it. Pastiche, self-parody, sudden shifts of tone and deliberate shock tactics, all came easily to one who had no settled respect for his own role, for his readers, or for the society in which the latter moved.

Was he, then, a satirist at all? F. R. Leavis compared him with Pope (whose poetry Byron idolised), and found in him an 'incapacity for Augustan satire', a lack of the requisite 'easy sureness of diction and tone, . . . neat precision and poise of movement and gesture, . . . elegant constancy of point, . . . even decorum'. *The Vision of Judgement*, Leavis wrote, succeeds because Byron has 'found a way of dispensing with these virtues'. Byron in that poem 'speaks as a man of the world and a gentleman, but not only is he not polite, the very essence of his manner is a contemptuous defiance of decorum and propriety'. Byron the satirist, Leavis suggests, 'has less affinity with Pope than with Burns'. A satirist must have a positive mind, contrasting with all his negatives: the positive to which Byron appeals is 'a generous common humanity, something that is indifferent to forms, conventions, and classes'. His 'satire' 'gets its characteristic effects by use of the irreverent familiar'.[18]

I think that Leavis was acute, yet made his definition of satire, so as to cover *The Vision*, too broad to be useful. That 'appeal to a generous common humanity' is found in writers within the conventions of realist fiction, but we do not call *Tom Jones* 'satire', nor do we apply the word to *Hard Times* or to *Vanity Fair*. Novelists habitually displayed 'familiar irreverence'.

Please now re-read *The Vision* and as you do so think about the questions just raised. How would you describe the diction, as compared with *Harold's*? How does Byron's chosen stanza form work? Would 'travesty', 'squib' or 'burlesque' suit the poem better than 'satire'?

DISCUSSION

Byron used the stanza which he had borrowed from the fifteenth-century Italian poet Pulci,[18] to use in his *Beppo* (1817), and had thereafter employed in *Don Juan*. Its challenge was to find enough rhymes for an *ababab* pattern – but it offered the pleasure of relaxation in a final couplet which could be used to punch an effect home. Byron's diction in the *Vision* remains, mostly, simple and sturdy. What marks it off from that of *Harold* is the freedom with which he brings in colloquialisms and slang. Taking just the first stanza: 'Not that the place by any means was full . . .', 'eighty-eight', 'a pull altogether' are expressions unfit either for Popeian satire, elevated Romantic discourse, or the rustic simplicity of a *Lyrical Ballad*. Yet such townee jargon appears alongside lines as impressively, traditionally poetic as any in Milton or Pope.

The first two lines occupy middle ground and establish a basic norm of diction – terse, plain and business-like. Byron, with notable economy, sets us down at a place, introduces a leading protagonist – *and* titillates our sense of the ridiculous. 'Saint Peter – celestial gate – rusty – dull': deadpan though the lines are, they hint at once at blasphemy.

But who is the arch-blasphemer? Byron's deadpan literalism implies that it is *Southey*. His original readers knew about Southey's poem, with its naively literal, tastelessly nationalistic description of the purlieus of heaven, and its equation of radicals with devils. Byron's implicit logic runs: '*If* my friend Leigh Hunt is a devil, when I know perfectly well that he's a rather sycophantic little man with an appalling wife and noisy brats, *then* the Other World is populated by creatures less exalted than we have imagined. *If* heaven is a kind of annexe of Whitehall and St Paul's Cathedral, *then* its gate-keeper must surely be a minor employee of the civil service. *If* salvation is dependent on politics, *then* (if Southey is right) most souls have been damned since the French Revolution infested Europe with radical ideas.'

The reduction of heaven to a bureaucracy is delightfully pointed in stanza III, when the recording angel is presented as a clerk maddened with business' so servile that he daren't ask his superiors for help, but maiming himself in the effort to keep up. The irony in line 27 is very neat. Earthly ministers are *of course* not 'cherubic' – therefore we know that Byron intends us to infer the opposite. Sure enough, the angelic clerks – a good-natured crew – cannot stomach the carnage which high-placed earthlings promote; the very devil himself is disgusted.

Consider now the treatment of George III himself in stanzas VIII–XII. How does Byron put down Southey here?


DISCUSSION

Byron introduces George III quite fair-mindedly: 'no tyrant', but a bad king. The transitions which follow, between stanzas VIII and XII, are brilliant. The pompous funeral is derided quite lightly – but in stanza X indignation swells *on behalf* of the dead king. The tables are turned on Southey and the Establishment, who value the institution, not the man. The couplet is as eloquent in its authority as any in English, with a hollow chime between 'mockery' and 'rottenness' generating immense power: what it implies is that the professed supporters of George III are in fact devilish in their callousness, an idea supported powerfully in XI. Men have a right to dissolve into the elements: the chemicals with which the king's body has been treated merely deface his natural humanity, shared with the 'mere million', ordinary people. XII resigns poor George to death with a gruff sigh – 'He's dead . . . He's buried . . . the world is gone/For him', as if he had been a rather difficult relation of the speaker. The stanza ends with a biting double irony. George III was, by implication, a fool, or at best, unlucky, to have been constant to a 'bad, ugly woman', but George IV is well known to lack the 'household virtue of constancy'. So much for Southey's conviction that the safety of the state depends on pure morality.

Stanzas XIII to XV mount a whirling attack, with outrageous rhymes, on the orthodox Christianity which Southey defended. They implicitly rebuke Christians for their lack of the supposedly Christian virtue of compassion. Do they *really* want sinners to suffer eternally? 'I may be damned, but at least I don't *want* my fellow creatures to fry.' Byron has brought us from this world back to the Other, of bliss and punishment. So we meet St Peter again, still dozing by his gate.

In the easy humour which now follows, 'the irreverent familiar' is dominant. Saints and angels and kings are cut down to size. St Peter himself turns out to be a kind of declassé aristocrat, jealous of the 'parvenu' St Paul, and, in his resentment, flirting with Jacobinism (stanza XXI).

The king's arrival, at last, is unimpressive; Southey hadn't understood that heaven, taken off guard like Whitehall suddenly faced by a crisis in some remote and forgotten colony, could hardly have mounted a show trial just like that. But Byron, the master of bathos, has a surprise for us. The amiably sluggish staff of heaven are suddenly confronted with the Devil.

Now please look at Byron's handling of Satan – and Michael – in stanzas XXIV–XLIX. What points is he using them to make? How does he characterise them? What transitions in tone do you detect?

DISCUSSION

The Devil turns out, aptly enough, to be a quintessential product of that Muse which Southey had termed 'Satanic'. He is the ultimate Byronic hero, with 'fierce and unfathomable thoughts', possessed by 'supernatural hate', a super-Napoleon frightening the angels, who, as Byron has learnt from Southey, are all Tories. And epically, to encounter this hero, forth from heaven comes the Tory champion. Michael arrives amid teasing irony. Byron can't describe him, because, as everyone knows (except the fanatic Southcote and the Laureate Southey), man can't see heavenly glory. Nevertheless, Byron implies, everyone seems to accept the versions of angels produced by poets and painters. Why would he be more blasphemous, in describing Michael, than some admired Old Master whose painting might hang on a nobleman's wall? A vengeful Calvinist lurks in these lines. Byron had been reared in a creed which, very logically, abhorred graven images. He mocks the muddled notions of would-be pious persons who don't, unlike well-versed Calvinists, grasp the logic of their own faith. How, for instance can saints and angels be 'young' or 'old' as we are on earth?

Irony of a simpler kind is also at work. 'Glory . . . good . . . goodly . . . glory . . . good . . . arch-angelic . . . angelical': repetition devalues the words of praise, until Byron skilfully resurects them by giving them a *human* content. When Michael and Satan meet, they remember 'good and ill' of each other. 'Good' is rescued from the tautology implicit in stanza XXX ('God is good, so good is what God does') and given its humanly right, relative meaning, such as we find through our experience ('That's not good for me').

Stanza XXXII is breathtaking. However one categorizes the whole poem, the effect here is certainly 'epic'. Byron evokes such a moment as the meeting of Napoleon and Wellington might have been. (Two opposing generals have all those things in common which they do not share with other beings – not least their keen rivalry.) But Calvinistic Byron goes beyond epic, to hint at the totalitarian predetermination, 'destiny', which Calvin's God had clamped on all sentient life, and from which even angels, logically, can't be exempt.

A conversational digression now lowers the tone, as it has to be lowered. Byron (line 272) reminds us again that Southey began this dubious procedure of writing literal-mindedly about heaven, as if 'accuracy' were possible. When they reappear, Satan and Michael are no longer epic heroes, but aristocratic grandees, evincing 'great politeness'. Michael's bow is a find thing – beyond modish foppery – but Satan's hauteur puts him in his place. The bureaucrat cannot match the hereditary master. Nevertheless, Byron gives Michael's speech in XXVIII a terse, Biblical-businesslike dignity, before Satan, the aristocratic rebel, takes over the poem.

And convinces St Peter. Satan's case, in XXIX–XLIX, is brilliantly argued. He cannot expect the Tory angels to sympathize with his sympathy for freedom – but surely they cannot forgive George III's opposition to Catholic Emancipation? Calvinist logic is on the war-path again, 'sub-textually'. Southey can't profess a literal-minded faith in a medieval, Catholic, 'un-Reformed' heaven with gates and angels, and oppose Emancipation (stanza XLVIII). The Church of England, which Southey serves, is hypocritical in offering a naively material heaven as compensation to the oppressed poor, while denying freedom of worship to 'primitive' Catholics.

Michael, alarmed by St Peter's Jacobinical outburst, hastens forward the witnesses. The teasing literal-mindedness which follows speaks for itself (here is the 'irreverent familiar' of which Leavis writes). Byron's Other World (stanzas LIX–LX) is riotously cosmopolitan, in deliberate contrast to Southey's English heaven. Michael, like Southey and other Tories, has clearly forgotten how much world exists. And so many damned souls pose a serious threat to law and order. The delicious stanza LXI describing Michael's discomfiture ('trout not stale' is a master-stroke) takes Southeyesque literalism to a supreme height of absurdity. Michael, however, does not cringe – he blandishes ('good old friend . . . my dear Lucifer'). Decorum is preserved. So Wilkes is called, in stanza LXV.

Unlike Southey's Wilkes, this one repents *nothing*. Byron characterizes him swiftly and brilliantly: the opportunism, the quick patter, the shock as he guesses the king is blind, the good-natured reluctance to attack a fallen enemy. Just as Wilkes in life evoked the equality of all Englishmen before the law, so here the law of heaven gives him scope to speak. Calvinist logic insists that a peer and a peasant may be equal before God; Southey's hierarchi-cally-minded Anglican friends have forgotten this fact, and have tried to pervert earthly justice in the interests of their class. But Wilkes's humane compassion annoys Satan, who suddenly loses his dignity and accuses him of conspiring with William Pitt. (A sweet touch, to have this Tory arch-hero basted in hell, with the fat of his corpulent Whig rival Fox, by his own mentor, Belial, whom all readers of Milton knew to be the most devious of devils. It was, we learn here, under Belial's tuition that Pitt put through the Alien and Sedition Acts of 1795 which severely restricted the freedom of the press.) Play follows upon the fact that nobody knew (or knows now) who wrote the famous Junius letters. Junius, unlike Wilkes, will give no quarter – but the trial, now going badly for George III, is mercifully interrupted by the arrival of Southey, the comic climax of the poem. Byron's details are very funny as they stand; funnier still if one can remember how Southey rose to heaven and fell in his own ponderous hexameters.

There is no need to comment on the gleeful skill with which Byron makes his vulture-faced homunculus destroy himself with his own vain mouth. He stands forth as the supreme hack (stanza C) with the most absurd pretensions (stanza CI). And yet, inadvertent-ly, Southey wins. Like the rubber heroes of farce, he is indestruc-tible. Sensible old St Peter, keeping his proletarian head while his superiors in office falter, knocks him down, but in vain. Byron expresses a truth which Gogol and Dostoevsky knew well: mediocrity (Russian, *poshlost*) is indestructible. Meanwhile, thanks to the chaos induced by Southey's hexameters, poor old George slips into heaven, to find a place among the sleepy choristers of that peaceful backwater.

We can now return to an earlier question. How does one classify this extraordinary poem? Please pause to take stock. It would be a good exercise to re-read stanzas IX–X, XVIII, XXXII and LV–LVI considering what term might best fit the character of each.


## DISCUSSION

The stanzas I mentioned are surely extremely varied, ranging from grave denunciation to light-hearted, flippant conversation. Critics have understandably been perplexed as to definitions. Bernard Blackstone, for one, can hardly disguise defeat. 'We are in the world of irony and farce, not of satire'.[19] For the surface of this text, 'burlesque' and 'travesty' are useful words. But they miss the poem's underlying seriousness. While Byron scores particular points off Southey, and his 'Vision', that bard's 'poetic felony "*de se*"' represents huge general targets: the vanity in both senses, of Anglican orthodoxy; the hypocrisy of most Christians, especially of those who use Christianity for the ends of a class; and the self-delusion of all who mystify earthly goings-on. The poem is as shocking – and as much in earnest – as Blake's *Marriage of Heaven and Hell*. The reader is challenged to recognize the pettiness of all wordly concerns *sub specie aeternitatis*, and to realize that true blasphemy consists of trivializing the cosmos, as Southey had done in his poem. Satan in his first grandeur (and even that is not sustained) is the only figure in the burlesque (farce? travesty?) who sets things in proportion, has the true measure of things. Granted that we are helpless before time and destiny, dwarfed by natural forces and by history, *still*, consciousness and reason, here given to Satan, are worth having, and offer such hope as we can possess of triumph, however temporary, for freedom.

The urbanity of Byron's poem, which implicitly rebukes the hysterical tone of Southey's attack on him, is not bolstered, like Pope's commanding voice, by a secure faith in hierarchy, a conviction that *x must* be better than *y*. It is, rather, a voice which Byron elects to assume for particular purposes, at a particular time – and is subject like any other voice which he might try out, to the devastating questions posed by his underlying secular-Calvinist consciousness. Captivated by *The Vision*, we're in the safe-seeming hands of a writer to whom there seemed to be no safety, part of whose spirit was carried forward by his admirer Matthew Arnold when the latter ended his *Dover Beach* (1867):

> Ah, love, let us be true
> To one another! for the world, which seems

To lie before us like a land of dreams,
So various, so beautiful, so new,
Hath really neither joy, nor love, nor light,
Nor certitude, nor peace, nor help for pain;
And we are here as on a darkling plain
Swept with confused alarms of struggle and flight,
Where ignorant armies clash by night.[21]

However, the Byron of *Don Juan*, unlike Arnold, could laugh in the face of all this. He must have heard in childhood that north-eastern Scottish song which recalls the last moments of the cattle-thief and fiddler James Macpherson, hanged at Banff in 1700.

Sae rantingly, sae wantonly,
  Sae dauntingly gae'd he,
He play'd a spring, and danc'd it round
  Below the gallows-tree.[22]

# 5. *Don Juan*

In August 1819 that well-known Tory journal *Blackwood's Edinburgh Magazine* published some 'Remarks on Don Juan', probably written by John Gibson Lockhart and John Wilson:

It has not been without much reflection and overcoming many reluctancies, that we have at last resolved to say a few words more to our readers concerning this very extraordinary poem ... in the composition of which there is unquestionably *a more thorough and intense infusion of genius and vice – power and profligacy – than in any poem which had ever before been written in the English, or indeed in any other modern language.* Had the wickedness been less inextricably mingled with the beauty and the grace, and the strength of a most inimitable and incomprehensible muse, our task would have been easy: But SILENCE would be a very poor and a very useless chastisement to be inflicted by us, or by any one, on a production, whose corruptions have been so effectually embalmed – which, *in spite of all that critics can do or refrain from doing, nothing can possibly prevent from taking a high place in the literature of our country, and remaining to all ages a perpetual monument of the exalted intellect, and the depraved heart, of one of the most remarkable men to whom that country has had the honour and the disgrace of giving birth.*

That Lord Byron has never written anything more decisively and triumphantly expressive of *the greatness of his genius*, will be allowed by all who have read this poem. That (laying all its manifold and grievous offences for a moment out of our view) it is *by far the most admirable specimen of the mixture of ease, strength, gayety, and seriousness extant in the whole body of English poetry*, is a proposition to which, we are almost as well persuaded, very few of them will refuse their assent. With sorrow and humiliation do we speak it – *the poet has devoted his powers to the worst of purposes and passions* . . .

The moral strain of the whole poem is pitched in the lowest key – and if the genius of the author lifts him now and then out of his pollution, it seems as if he regretted the elevation, and made all haste to descend again. To particularize the offences committed in its pages would be worse than vain – because the *great genius of the man* seems to have been throughout exerted to its utmost strength, in devising every possible method of pouring scorn upon every element of good or noble nature in the hearts of his readers. Love – honour – patriotism – religion, are mentioned only to be scoffed at and derided, as if their sole resting-place were, or ought to be, in the bosoms of fools. It appears, in short, as if *this miserable man*, having exhausted every species of sensual gratification – having drained the cup of sin even to its bitterest dregs, were resolved to shew us that he is no longer a human being, even in his frailties; – but *a cool unconcerned fiend*, laughing with a detestable glee over the whole of the better and worse elements of which human life is composed – treating well nigh with equal derision the most pure of virtues, and the most odious of vices – dead alike to the beauty of the one, and the deformity of the other – a mere heartless despiser of that frail but noble humanity, whose type was never exhibited in a shape of more *deplorable degradation* than in his own contemptuously distinct delineation of himself . . .

It has long been sufficiently manifest, that this man is devoid of religion. At times, indeed, the power and presence of the Deity, as speaking in the sterner workings of the elements, seems to force some momentary consciousness of their existence into his labouring breast; – *a spirit in which there breathes so much of the divine, cannot always resist the majesty of its Maker.* But of true religion terror is a small part – and of all religion, that founded on mere terror, is the least worthy of such a man as Byron. We may look in vain through all his works for the slightest evidence that his soul had ever listened to the gentle voice of the oracles. The same proud hardness of heart which makes the author of Don Juan a despiser of the Faith for which his fathers bled, has rendered him a scorner of

the better part of woman; and therefore it is that his love poetry is a
continual insult to the beauty that inspires it. The earthy part of the
passion is all that has found a resting place within his breast. . . .

What *are* we to make – what was anyone *ever* to make – of
*Blackwood's* mystical construction of something called 'genius'
which may exist as a kind of absolute spiritual force in a being
utterly depraved? The critic puts himself into the absurd position of
consigning *Juan* to the flames of hell while acknowledging that it is
a masterpiece. One does not have to be either a Calvinist or a
Marxist to reject such besotted 'bourgeois' idealism.

Byron had hit his target, the *Blackwood's* mentality. *Don Juan*
caused a furore and flushed out its author's enemies. Byron fought
his battles in a period of transition between the values of
Enlightenment thought and those of an emergent high 'Victorian'
frame of mind.

Kelvin Everest has usefully discussed the rise of this frame of
mind, which he identifies with 'classic bourgeois values', in relation
to certain features of British national culture in particular.[2] From
the 1780s, Evangelical Christianity gained increasing influence
within the churches and over public life. It is important to note that
its theology (which was intellectually somewhat lax) had nothing in
common with the rigorous Calvinist tradition. But the morality of
Wilberforce and such co-adjutors as Hannah More was sternly
'puritanical'. I have already pointed to the Evangelicals' role in
securing sterner enforcement of the law against male homosexual
practices. Meanwhile, in economic theory, 'a quasi-scientific
rationalization of the values of industrial and mercantile capitalism
was presented as an account of natural laws at work within the
economy'. In the 1980s we should have a pretty keen sense of what
was involved here. *Laissez-faire* theory deprecated as sentimental
old fashioned paternalism in relations between employer and
employee. The Luddites whose cause Byron espoused in the House
of Lords were amongst many victims of the new way of thinking. It
interacted complexly, however, with the movement for political
reform – the widening of the franchise to include more of the
middle classes – which triumphed in 1832 and can be seen as
'democratizing'. One could be a 'radical' wholly convinced by
*laissez-faire* economics, and sympathetic towards both Evangelicalism and political reform. But Byron, like his friend Shelley and
Shelley's friend Peacock, was a writer aligned with radicalism
though harking back to the eighteenth-century Enlightenment, with
its pronounced tendency to reject Christianity.

While much 'Enlightened' thought – Voltaire's and Gibbon's,
for instance – was explicitly anti-democratic, some had a demo-

cratic direction (Rousseau's, Jefferson's). Tom Paine, arch-fiend in Tory demonology, carried the Enlightenment frame of mind into full approval of egalitarianism, as did Burns in his famous line, 'a man's a man for a' that'. Both went further than Byron ever did, but aristocratic Enlightenment *reasoning* might see no *rational* basis for the conventional distinction between prince and peasant. It might apply a very sharp cutting-edge indeed to all hierarchies, in Church and State. It was tolerant in its view of sexual behaviour.

Kelvin Everest rightly stresses the 'disconcerting interchange of arguments and attitudes', in the Romantic period, between 'actually opposed political interests.'[3] Byron himself was in some respects 'bourgeois'. The emergent 'Victorian' ideological cluster incorporated elements of Enlightenment thinking – the economics of Adam Smith, above all, and the rationalizing ideas of Jeremy Bentham in administration. It was not necessarily anti-egalitarian. Evangelical Christianity, after all, insisted on the equality of all souls, including those of black slaves, before God, and many campaigners against slavery were anti-hierarchical and anti-feudal in their emphases. But what many left-wing 'bourgeois' thinkers had in common with Tories like Southey was an intense moral earnestness, a faith in the family and in 'domestic' values, a pompous conviction that the most important people in the world were persons of white, 'Anglo-Saxon' stock, to whom God or economic necessity had given moral custody over the rest. To such left-wing, 'reforming' persons the inhabitants of Spain and Italy, so attractive to Byron, were suspect because they were idle and slovenly. To the Tory bourgeois, they were branded with the twin stigmata of Catholicism and sexual laxity.

All full-blown variants of 'bourgeois' thought mystified 'art'. In the mid-eighteenth century the word 'genius' meant 'talent'. To say that a man had a 'great genius' was merely to say that he was very talented. If he misapplied his talent, this was one of the accidents of life; and if social conditions frustrated his 'genius', this was bad luck. No *impiety* was involved in either case. But by 1819 *Blackwood's* is using the term superstitiously. Genius is 'exalted', it partakes of the divine. Byron, the review implies, has been fulfilling a kind of sacred mission in his earlier poetry. The reviewer remarks bitterly that 'Every high thought that was ever kindled in our breasts by the name of Byron – every pure and lofty feeling that ever responded from within us to the sweep of his majestic inspirations – every remembered moment of admiration and enthusiasm is up in arms against him'.[4]

In so far as a younger Byron had connived in the creation of 'Byronism', he had contributed to the bourgeois cult of the 'genius'.

Why did 'bourgeois' thought deify the poet's 'individual genius' while accepting, and even *enforcing*, his separateness from society? Why did the (surely pernicious) myth arise that poetry has nothing to do with everyday life, but is holy and apart? Both Benthamite liberal and Tory bourgeois had an interest, unconscious or semi-conscious, in creating such a myth.

To the Adam Smith-ite or Bentham-ite reformer, everything which was not 'useful' ('use' being defined in economic terms) must be excluded from the sphere in which commerce, manufacture and statecraft worked out their 'progressive' destinies. Literature was acceptable *only* as a 'serious' recreation, as a necessary safety-valve for feelings and imaginings which might otherwise interfere with business. Meanwhile, the Evangelical or Tory Churchman could accept poetry only as a handmaid to 'pure', that is to 'religious', feeling. Wordsworth's poetry was increasingly acceptable because it derived from a kind of religious experience in an area, 'the Lakes', which was remote from the more blatant manifestations of industrialization, and thus easy to mystify.

*Don Juan* was directed, by an on-the-whole repentant 'Byron-ist', against the whole 'bourgeois' ideological cluster in which the Toryism of Castlereagh overlapped with aspects of 'Laker' religious feeling, with Evangelicalism, and with the interest of manufacturers in controlling the pleasures of the poor. Industry needed a disciplined workforce. Sex, and pleasure in general, were bad for discipline. This period saw the beginnings of a massive attack by the ruling classes on fairs, wakes, rowdy sports and popular amusements. Traditionally, sections of the aristocracy had patron-ized and even shared in such amusements – thus, Byron had spent a lot of time with boxers. In revolt against the bourgeois cast of thought which was now beginning to infect even his own class, the peerage, with what he called 'cant', Byron was striking at a cluster of ideological discourses in which religion, economics, and sexual-ity were complexly related together. The editors of *Blackwood's* were understandably horrified, although, as clever literary men themselves, they were bound to admire Byron's skill.

It is relevant here to mention three novels from the eighteenth century Enlightenment: Fielding's *Tom Jones*; Voltaire's *Candide*; and Laclos's *Liaisons dangereuses*. I think they help to explain, as 'Augustan traditions of satire' do not, many salient features of *Don Juan*.

Byron admired Fielding extremely. He called him 'the prose Homer of human nature' ('Ravenna Journal', 1821), and reckoned that he would have been branded a 'revolutionist' by current Tories ('Detached Thoughts', 1821–2).[5] Tom Jones is a bastard, who gets

involved in a series of extra-marital sexual adventures. Nevertheless, he is a true 'hero'; the reader is led to see his essential good-
heartedness as intrinsically superior to the systematic moralizing of
bigoted and hypocritical Christians, represented by his tutor
Thwackum. Byron's debt to Voltaire is obvious; both men use
irony with a boisterous zest for demystification, and *Juan* has
significant affinities with the French free-thinker's famous tale,
*Candide* (which might be described as a comic strip in ironic prose).
In both cases, a sharp point is made about the defectiveness of the
hero's education in equipping him for real life. In both cases,
recurrent themes are projected as the young hero wanders from
country to country, posted forward by surprising accidents,
preserved by improbable escapes from death. Like Voltaire, Byron
exercises his wit, and moralizes, about mankind in a variety of
climes, while reserving his most deadly shafts for his own
homeland. Finally, Byron had read Laclos's novel. In a diary of
1813 he echoes with sympathy a dictum which he mis-attributes to
Valmont: 'One gets tired of everything, my angel.' In fact this is
quoted in the novel by Valmont's former mistress, the Marquise;
but the fascinating Valmont, a cynic devoted to seduction yet truly
allured by the chaste woman whom he pursues, is a prototype for
the 'Byronic' hero.[6] *Don Juan* shares with *Les liaisons dangereuses*
the perception that sexuality is at the centre of social relationships.
To write 'realistically' about sex will expose important features of
society in general which otherwise are ignored or mystified.

I'm arguing that an 'Enlightened' cast of mind supplanted, in
*Juan*, the Romantic Byronism of the shorter tales and of *Childe
Harold*, and that the mode of *Juan* is not, overall, 'satirical', but
'realistic'. It is sharply differentiated from the 'Augustan' verse
satire of Pope and Churchill (much though that influenced Byron)
by its explicit abandonment of a stable, 'classical', hierarchical set
of values. The poem does not appeal to our sense of what is right. It
appeals to our sense of *fact*, what is 'real'. It rests its case on
observation, and is 'moral' in so far as Byron subscribes to the
implicit credo of fictional 'realism', that the world, and human
nature, must be confronted *as they are*, if we are to improve life.

As Byron puts it, in Canto 12, of *Juan*, stanza XL:

> But now I'm going to be immoral, now
> > I mean to show things really as they are,
> Not as they ought to be, for I avow,
> > That till we see what's what in fact, we're far
> From much improvement with that virtuous plough
> > Which skims the surface, leaving scarce a scar

> Upon the black loam long manured by vice,
> Only to keep its corn at the old price.[7]

The imagery here associates moral improvement with material progress. 'If we can plough deeper into man's nature, which, as all Calvinizers know, is black and sinful, it will yield *material* benefit – richer "harvests", cheaper "corn".' Like his friend and hero Scott, and unlike the Lakers, Byron was comfortable with the idea of material 'improvement' so much in the air in his day. He did not reject the positive aspects of industrialism – rather, he seems to have taken them for granted. But he denounced (as in his speech on the Luddites in the House of Lords) the *cant* of the classes who presided over industrialization. He was friendly towards *some* bourgeois values, but deeply antipathetic to the mystifications of emergent 'Victorianism'. By 1819 the increasing influence of Evangelicalism, and the increasingly explicit connexion drawn by bourgeois thinkers between sexual freedom and social disorder, made *Juan*'s very publication problematic.

Byron began work on *Don Juan* early in July 1818. His correspondents in London were soon in consternation. His friend and agent, Hobhouse, confided to his diary after he first saw the poem: 'I have my doubts about "Don Juan"; the blasphemy and bawdry ... overpower even the great genius it displays.' Other friends of the poet joined Hobhouse in advising Murray, the publisher, against touching it; even the easy-going Moore thought it 'as a whole not publishable'. Byron retored with several different lines of argument:

1 Chaucer, Shakespeare, etc. had been just as indelicate.
2 *Juan* was in fact 'the most moral of poems' (so he told Murray); 'but if people won't discover the moral, that is their fault, not mine.'
3 The poem should be judged on its merits as a poem – decency was neither here nor there.
4 Society was as he described it; he was merely being 'realistic'.
5 'A complex, confused resurgence of *Childe Harold's* self-dramatization': he claimed to be indifferent to the public's opinion and heartily ready to have a fight with it, 'a war of criticism and methodism'.[8]

Byron was prepared to use any and every possible argument on *Juan's* behalf because he believed that he was writing well. But even after he prevailed over Murray and his London friends, so that the first two cantos (but MINUS the Dedication) came out in July 1819, he had further discouragements to surmount.

He would not have been surprised or dismayed to learn that Wordsworth was urging the *Quarterly Review* to attack *Juan* – not by a 'formal Critique', which would help publicize it, but by a

direct attack on its 'damnable tendency'. ('What avails it to hunt
down Shelley, whom few read, and leave Byron untouched?'
Wordsworth asked. 'I am persuaded that *Don Juan* will do more
harm to the English character, than anything of our time . . .') But
he cannot have been pleased to find Leigh Hunt, who defended the
poem in a published review, conceding nevertheless that he found it
'extremely unpleasant and mortifying' when Byron turned 'all the
fine ideas' he had excited to 'ridicule and hopelessness'. Shelley
wrote to him with high praise; he thought parts of Canto 2 almost
equal to Dante, and was fulsome about his friend's psychological
insights ('Where did you learn all these secrets? I should like to go to
school there'). But even Shelley politely said that he did not
'altogether think the bitter mocking of our common nature . . .
quite worthy of your genius'. Keats threw down the book in
disgust, shocked that Byron should 'laugh & gloat over the most
solemn & heart-rending scenes of human misery'. That unease over
Byron's poem must have been almost general is shown by a letter to
him from the famous courtesan Harriet Wilson:

> Dear *Adorable* Lord Byron, *don't* make a mere *coarse* old libertine of
> yourself. . . . When you don't feel quite up to a spirit of benevolence
> . . . in *gratitude* for the talent which, after all, must have caused you
> exquisite moments in your time, throw away your pen, my love, and
> take a little *calomel*. I wish the Deuce had all the paper, pens and ink
> burning, frizzling and drying up in the very hottest place in his
> dominions, rather than you should use them to wilfully destroy the
> respect and admiration of those who deserve to love you and all the
> fine illusions with which my mind was filled. Écoutez, mon Ange.[9]

In hitting his target, the *Blackwood's* mentality, with such
precision, Byron had scattered shrapnel enough to wound those
most sympathetic to him. His mistress, the Countess Guiccioli,
persuaded him to stop writing more *Juan*, in July 1821, after he had
completed Canto 5. Her arguments, according to him, were those
of women readers in general. 'Women all over the world,' he wrote,
'always retain their Free masonry – and as that consists in the
illusion of the Sentiment – which constitutes their sole empire . . .
all works which refer to the *comedy* of the passions – & laugh at
the Sentimentalism – of course are proscribed by the whole *Sect*
[sex]'.[10]

But he returned to *Juan* after a year. Murray declined to
publish any more, so Byron gave further instalments to Leigh
Hunt's brother, John, who published Cantos 6 to 14 in the second
half of 1823, and Cantos 15 and 16 early in 1824, a bare three
weeks before his death. The tale stops abruptly, unfinished.

After Inez despatches Juan from Cadiz, Canto 2 involves him in a shipwreck and terrible experiences on an open boat, where other survivors resort to cannibalism. This at last runs ashore on a Greek island, where Juan, washed up on the sand, is discovered by Haidée, daughter of the place's pirate ruler, Lambro. His love-idyll with this unspoilt but sensuous beauty is tragically shattered by her father's return (Cantos 3 and 4). Haidée dies in a kind of fit and Juan is shipped off for sale in the slave market in Constantinople.

Canto 5 introduces him, now a possession of Ottoman Sultan, to the imperious Sultana Gulbeyaz, whose haughty advances prompt him to an impassioned assertion of his independence – 'our souls at least are free'. He escapes (Canto 6) after some low jinks in the harem, which he enters dressed as a woman, and flees towards the border (Cantos 7 and 8), where he joins the Russians in their bloody siege and capture of the town of Ismail. He fights bravely in the battle, but Byron denounces war so fiercely that his hero seems compromised. To show that Juan retains his good nature, Byron has him insist on saving an orphan child from death, and this girl, Leila, accompanies him on his further travels. He arrives as a military hero in the court of Catherine the Great of Russia, and the ageing empress makes him her reluctant paramour. The Russian cantos, 9 and 10, seem disappointingly shallow after what has preceded them, but they fulfill the narrative function of transforming Juan from a naive and impressionable lad into a man of the world, fit to be sent by Catherine on a mission to England. English society, mostly 'high' society, is directly in Byron's sights during the remainder of the poem.

From remarks made to his publisher in 1821 it appears that Byron at that stage thought of making Juan 'cause for a divorce' in England and taking him to Italy and to Germany where he would cut a 'sentimental' figure in the Werther style. He might die in the French Revolution, go to Hell or – worse! – get married.[11] We must doubt whether Byron had any settled grand plan, even in his head, but clearly the character of the poem was to remain much as it had been in Canto 1. While it would display the absurdities of life in a succession of countries its story-line would stay, for all its wealth of digressive topical reference, firmly within the eighteenth century. It's rather as if Byron's later admirer W. H. Auden had chosen to comment on the society of the 1930s through a tale set around the turn of the century and ending with the First World War. While passages in *Juan* may be 'satirical' in flavour, such a project was hardly one for 'satire' as the word is usually understood.

In 1818, Byron drafted a prose preface to Cantos 1 and 2 which remained unpublished till 1901.[12] He began with characteris-

tic jibes at Wordsworth's 'trash' and 'prosaic raving', and alluded
to that poet's asking his readers to imagine that his little story 'The
Thorn' was spoken by a retired sea captain:

> The reader ... is requested to suppose by a like exericse of
> imagination that the following epic narrative is told by a Spanish
> gentleman in a village in the Sierra Morena on the road between
> Monasterio and Seville, sitting at the door of a *posada* (inn) with the
> Curate of the hamlet on his right hand, a cigar in his mouth, a jug of
> Malaga or perhaps 'right sherris' before him on a small table ... The
> time, sunset. At some distance a group of black-eyed peasantry are
> dancing to the sound of the flute. ...

Byron goes on to add further details to a lively cosmopolitan scene
– foreign gentlemen are present, French prisoners of war in the
offing – in a charming evocation of the sunlit Mediterranean
ambience with which he had fallen in love in his earliest travels in
Iberia during the Peninsular War. But he knows that he can't
convincingly place his narrator in it. How is it that the Spanish
gentleman speaks English?

> The reader is further requested to suppose him ... either an
> Englishman settled in Spain, or a Spaniard who had travelled in
> England ... Having supposed as much of this as the utter
> impossibility of such a supposition will admit, the reader is requested
> to extend his supposed power of supposing so far as to conceive that
> the dedication to Mr Southey and several stanzas of the poem itself
> are interpolated by the English editor.

Even with the 'Dedication' left out, the persona of the narrator
of Canto 1 remains unstable. By the end of the Canto, the worldly-
wise Spanish gentleman has evaporated even more thoroughly than
Childe Harold did.

Byron was convinced that he was making important moral and
political statements in *Juan*. In 1822, he would write rather
grandiosely to friends that he was fighting a battle for 'philosophy' against 'tyranny' for the 'good of mankind', and would not
be prevented by any 'outcry' against his poem 'from telling the
tyrants who (were) attempting to trample upon all thought, that
their thrones will yet be rocked to their foundation.'[13] But his
weapons in his battle were improvisation and apparent spon-
taneity. His technique in *Juan* – the stanza form itself, the
freewheeling digressions, the variations in diction and tone – were
in themselves a teasing challenge to pompous, 'canting', orthodox
persons.

The first readers of *Juan* would have identified the 'voice' of stanza I as Byron's own, but would have been teased (as we still are) by the shift of the narrative voice from that of omniscient 'epic' poet to minor comic participant in the action. Please now read Canto 1, considering, as you do so, Byron's narrative *persona* – or *personae*. Where do you find shifts in voice and in point of view?

## DISCUSSION

The first seven stanzas introduce a highly self-conscious authorial voice, for which Byron had a precedent in the 'essays' which Fielding had interspersed in his narrative of *Tom Jones*.

That this voice is tongue-in-cheek is established at once. We do not yet know that Byron's Don Juan is to be vastly different from Mozart's and from the Juan of 'pantomime' – he will be a basically good-hearted young man, not a cynical roué, a cross between Tom Jones and Candide, not a Valmont. But by the end of stanza II, any alert reader would sense a leg-pull. The speaker brackets the great Buonaparté with the relatively obscure Dumourier and implies that *both* owed their fame to the press. The outrageous rhymes of 'Agamemnon/same none/condemn none' in stanza V undermine all the epic pretensions which the speaker then playfully assumes, and we would be fools to trust such a narrator when he claims (in stanza VII) 'regularity' for his design.

So we are prepared for the clowning descent of the speaker, so urbanely knowledgeable about English society ('Feinagle', 'Miss Edgeworth's novels') into the persona of a 'plain' Spanish bachelor in a 'single station', a busybody who gets doused with water by mischievous young Juan.

By stanza XXXIV his omniscience is definitely gone ('so they say ... I ask'd'), and by XLVIII and LI–LIII he's being further 'characterized' as a fussy, sly fellow. We have been drawn into a world where gossip and slander make truth hard to discover; and this involves indirect assault by the poet on the English society which gossiped about him.

But the speaker wants to establish his claim to be *factual*. In stanza CIII, 'I like to be particular in dates' advertises more than it might at first seem to. The ironic thrust of the passage which follows and takes us on to Julia's 'fall' in CXVII is against those who deny 'facts' and prefer 'illusions' (as Byron protested all women did). What shocked *Blackwood's*, and troubled even Shelley, were the pains which Byron took to demystify the very passion, love, which his verse tales had seemed to exalt.

Please now look at the movement in tone in stanza CVI, and consider the effect which Byron achieves in the last two lines.

## DISCUSSION

Julia, over-confident, deceives herself. Juan has been left entirely vulnerable to her allure by his education. This was designed (stanza XXXIX) to make him 'strictly moral' – and therefore omitted 'natural history' and the 'facts of life'. The opening of stanza CVI is ardent, the close is curt. Dry short 'e's emphasize the irony of the final couplet, and prepare us for the generalized cynicism of stanza CVIII.

He falls in love (stanzas LXXXVI–XCVI) without any realistic grasp of the basis of his emotions. And Byron teases not only those who take their notions of love from the poet Campbell (quoted in LXXXVIII) and are hoaxed by the mysteries announced by Words-worth and Coleridge (XCI), but also admirers of his own *Childe Harold*. All such fine sentiments mystify the facts of life: Juan is *instinctively* drawn to gratify his sexual impulse (by CXVII). As we are eloquently told in CXVI, to fantasize about 'pure' love like a *Blackwood's* critic is really to propagate 'immorality'. Such fantasies lure Julia and Juan into a sexual liaison of ill-assorted ages, dangerous to both, destructive for Julia.

Please now consider stanzas CXXXII to CXXXIII again. They form an elaborate digression, splitting the canto roughly in half. What point do you find in their shifts of tone? And can you summarize the 'argument' from CXXVIII on, steering round any topical allusions which puzzle you and going for the general sense?

## DISCUSSION

Stanzas CXXII and CXXIII are pleasantly lyrical – such sentiments would seem 'exalted' enough to a 'bourgeois' reviewer. Byron then plunges deliciously into bathos. But he is not asserting that moonlight in Venice and the 'lisp of children' *aren't* pleasurable, merely reminding us that humankind is various in its tastes. Rhetoric, whether Romantic or epic, can't cope with such banal facts of human nature as the pleasure we can take in quarreling with 'a tiresome friend'. Old wine, a fit subject for 'poetry' since it features in the Greek and Roman classics is, after all, not unlike 'ale' in its effect. And, completely to unsettle his readers, Byron

### CANTO I, ST. 158

1 She ceased & turned upon her pillow;—pale

2 ~~But beautiful she lay—her eyes shed tears~~
       ~~lays~~
       ~~lies~~
       ~~lays,~~    ~~lies~~
            ~~the starting tears~~
            ~~and drop the tears~~

3 ~~Reluctant past her bright eyes rolled—as a veil~~

4 ~~Like Summer rains through Sunshine~~
  ~~As~~         ~~drop~~
         ~~flow fastly~~

3 ~~From her bright eyes reluctant rolled the veil~~
         ~~flows as a veil~~
         ~~leaps~~

4 ~~Of her dishevelled tresses dark appears~~
     ~~dark dishevelled tresses~~

5 ~~Wooing her cheek—the~~  ~~dar~~  ~~black curls strive but fail~~
  ~~Contrasting with her cheek—& bosom~~
         ~~they~~
      ~~her~~  ~~& strive but fail~~ [3]

2 She lay, her dark eyes flashing through their tears,

3 ~~As~~ Like Skies that rain and lighten; as a veil

4 Waved and ~~oerflowing~~ her wan cheek appears
    oershading

5 Her ~~hair~~ streaming hair—the black curls strive but fail

6 To hide the glossy shoulder which ~~still~~ uprears

7 ~~It's symmetry with~~
~~In shining~~
~~It's whiteness through them all—with lips~~
It's snow through all—~~she lay with soft lips~~
       ~~her~~  ~~lips~~  ~~sweet lips lay apart~~
         ~~ripe lips lie apart~~
    her soft lips lie apart.

8 And louder than her breathing beats her heart.

*Reworking by Byron of* Don Juan, *Canto 1, stanza* CLVIII, *from* Truman Guy Steffan *(ed.),* The Making of a Masterpiece (Byron's 'Don Juan': A Variorum Edition, *vol. 1), University of Texas Press, 1957, 1971, page 341. (Copyright © 1957, 1971 The University of Texas Press)*

follows this sensible implication with 'straight' enough evocations of 'Romantic' chivalry and 'Romantic' nostalgia, modulating towards the resounding, terse, carefully measured statement in stanza CXXVII of his secular-Calvinist vision. 'Really', sex, while 'sinful', is, in its first and freshest experience, 'ambrosial'. It is, implicitly, worth struggle, tragic struggle, like the 'fire which Prometheus filched for us from heaven', for which deed on behalf of humanity God punished him so dreadfully.

This in turn leads our practically-minded narrator to think of current heirs of Prometheus, the inventors of his own day. The common-sense, cheerful acceptance of useful devices is cut across by a thought about the 'great' pox, syphilis, which carries us into a grimly ironic stanza about America. Byron was an admirer of the USA. Its burgeoning frontier, its limitless expanses, supported, as he knew, a rapidly growing population. The sombre theorizings of the political economist Malthus argued that human population could expand only up to a given point before famine and disease acted as a natural corrective. The poor, as hard bourgeois thinkers argued, were foolish to breed so rapidly; if the Irish starved, it was their own fault. But in America Byron saw cause for an optimism to contradict bourgeois repressiveness masquerading as 'natural history'. The Americans, he ironically implies, are exempt from our 'civilization's 'pseudo-syphilis' ('syphilization'). The last line of this stanza suggests that the *real* disease native to the New World and contracted through sexual intercourse is preferable to the bogey-diseases conjured up by Malthusians, and by the kind of Christian moralist who tries to frighten people away from sex by the threat of VD. Evangelicals have produced (stanza CXXXII) 'new inventions' for 'saving souls', but do not condemn the hideous carnage of Waterloo and other ('civilized/syphilized') battlefields.

Having thus attacked misuse of political power and sexual repressiveness simultaneously, and questioned whether either is truly 'civilized', Byron urbanely presents the horrific thought that there may be no after-life. And if there is no hell-fire, Christian threats against pleasurable 'sin' lose all their force.

The *dénouement* of the Canto might suggest 'bedroom farce', but I think its effects are closer to those of comic opera. Please now refer to the reproduction on p. 77, of T. G. Steffan's presentation of the main changes which Byron made in his drafts of stanza CLVIII. Steffan believes that at this point Byron, despite some pains – his air of careless improvisation was assumed – failed here 'to achieve the sensuous, pathetic effect he laboured for.'[14] What do you think? Would such an effect be appropriate, in view of the previous twenty-two stanzas? What effect is actually achieved by the words 'flashing', 'streaming' and 'uprears'?

DISCUSSION

I think that Byron may have realized as he worked that he shouldn't make Julia 'pathetic' here. Discarded lines do suggest an initial attempt at pathos. Julia 'shedding' tears, or tears 'rolling' from her eyes, imply a woman involuntarily overcome. 'Her dark eyes flashing through her tears', however, and the 'uprearing' of her shoulder indicate that she is on the *qui vive*, as we would expect of a woman with her lover concealed in bed beside her, who has just, over thirteen stanzas, delivered a wonderful diatribe against her husband, revealing, in much comic detail, her consciousness of her own sexual allure. 'Streaming' and 'glossy' emphasize her fullness of life in a somewhat exaggerated way. She is 'dramatizing herself', and she is no innocent subject for readers' sentimental tears:

> Is it for this I scarce went anywhere,
> Except to bull-fights, mass, play, rout and revel?

It is useful to mention Mozart's Cherubino again here. In comic opera characters can sing lovely arias and yet be found in ludicrous situations. Julia is a magnificent-looking woman (and also a good-natured one), but Juan's shoes will shortly be her come-uppance. And though even after that Byron will move us with her Letter to Juan (stanzas XCII–CXCVII), which may be compared in effect to an aria, he will return her to commonplace humanity with the dry observation:

> This note was written upon gilt-edged paper
> With a neat little crow-quill, slight and new . . .

How can one square the assertion that Byron's conceives his Julia 'operatically' with his narrator's claim that his story's 'actually true'? This claim, made by a *persona* who more than a hundred lines back said 'Here ends this canto', is to be taken as teasing, tongue in cheek. Yet the appeal to truth, as I've already suggested, is central to the import of *Don Juan*. Is his projection of human nature compatible with his ambition to show things as they 'really are'?

Yes, if we get away from the idea that a human being is all of a piece, that valuable people must always be taken seriously, that only serious people are valuable. Against this notion, Julia might be said to exhibit the 'truth' that we find in Mozart's operas and, for that matter, in Shakespeare's *Antony and Cleopatra*, that indivi-dual human beings have potential both for comedy and pathos. The narrator conceives himself this way, as we see from the famous, digressive lament for lost youth which aptly concludes a canto in which two highly attractive young people have enjoyed high pleasure together, yet have made fools of themselves and have been punished.

Please now consider the effect of shifts of tone in stanzas CCXIII to CCXIX. How would you characterize the speaker here? A comfortable, wise, Spanish gentleman . . . ?


## DISCUSSION

After a bluff, businesslike broaching of the topic ('forty' – 'in short, 1') in stanza CCXIII, the narrator surprises us with fulsome poetry, a high-Romantic lament for the 'freshness of the heart', which modulates deliciously in stanza CCXV to land with a bump in the half-rhyme of 'judgment' with 'lodgement'. The next stanza is skittishly cynical, reducing love and even friendship to the 'credulous hope of mutual minds'. Yet CCXVII beings with two resonant Childe Harold-like lines. Love may be over, but at least the speaker can take his own despair seriously? Not if it's pitched as high as this. The prosaic 'two last' in the next line begins to undermine grandiosity. I think at this moment not of a cheery Spanish gentleman but of a man fatally self aware, too intelligent for his own good, relieving himself of strong feelings to a confidential friend who knows him too well not to see through his postures.

But a further modulation brings in a tone which seems immune to the friend's sad smile, ¯aised eyebrows. Stanza CCXVIII projects a 'sincere' world-weariness, in the spirit of secular Calvinism. *Reason* tells us that poetry and literary fame are as transient as passion. Yet the vista of the world is not entirely bleak when we have intelligence which can apply to fate and its accidents a shoulder-shrugging but self-delighted wit. 'We've all had it, but we don't need to make fools of ourselves bidding for immortality like the pyramid-building pharaoh King Cheops.'

The remainder of *Don Juan* (which I hope you will find time to read) shows that Byron himself was certainly not out to create a structure like a pyramid – regular in form, solid, monumental. His largest and (most think) best work is fluid as sparkling wine. 'I meant to make this poem very short/But now I can't tell where it may not run', Byron exclaims in the twenty-second stanza of Canto 15. (This is on page 502, no less, of the Penguin edition; page numbers from now on refer to this edition.[15]) *Juan*, in the words of Jerome J. McGann, 'gathered its form about itself in the course of its composition', and could have gone on doing so indefinitely had

Byron's death not interrupted it fourteen stanzas into Canto 17. McGann stresses 'the tentative, "preliminary" character of the poem, as if its literal "execution" on the page involved an "execution" in both senses, of the preliminary design, as if the poem were constantly revising itself and canceling previous intentions (which, however, it might at any point return to).' He points out that Byron himself called *Juan* an 'experiment' and that each of its episodes – McGann tentatively numbers them at ten, but the flow is such that this is problematic – involves quasi-'scientific' experiment with new materials, questioning conventional ideas from new positions.[16]

The shifts of tone which we have witnessed between sections, and even within stanzas of Canto 1 are also experienced between episodes. Nothing in the first canto has prepared us for the shipwreck scene in the second. Two hundred or so perish: thirty survive in a longboat, among them Juan and his tutor Pedrillo. Also Juan's pet spaniel. Food soon runs out. After the spaniel has been devoured, cannibalism seems the only recourse and Julia's letter is taken by force from Juan and torn up to make lots. Pedrillo is the unlucky man. The medical man present bleeds him to death (Canto 2, stanza 77, page 121).

> The surgeon, as there was no other fee,
> Had his first choice of morsels for his pains,
> But being thirstiest at the moment, he
> Preferred a draught from the fast-flowing veins.
> Part was divided, part thrown in the sea,
> And such things as the entrails and the brains
> Regaled two sharks who followed o'er the billow.
> The sailors ate the rest of poor Pedrillo.

'Bathos' seems not quite the right word for the effect of the final rhyme there, or for similar two-syllable rhymes elsewhere in this episode, of which:

> They grieved for those who perished with the cutter,
> And also for the biscuit casks and butter.

> (Stanza 61, page 117)

struck Byron's *Blackwood* critics as 'the most innocent of all his odious sarcasms' regarding the shipwreck.[17] The narrative is terse and straightforward. The double rhymes have a throwaway air, enhancing its matter-of-factness. Byron is enforcing on his readers the recognition that the survivors are not uniquely evil people, but typical of the human race. Under such conditions, fine feelings are unlikely to prevail, since (stanza 67, page 118) '. . . Man is a carnivorous production/And must have meals, at least one meal a day.'

Juan's exceptional good nature has been shown by his refusing to eat more than half a forepaw of his dog, or any of his tutor. But when Haidée, having rescued him, returns full of love, her maid prudently fries eggs, knowing that 'the best feelings must have victual' – and of course Juan duly falls on the food offered him like 'A priest, a shark, an alderman or pike'. (Stanzas 145 and 157, pages 138 and 141.)

However, despite such insistent realism and despite irreverent digressions ('Man being reasonable must get drunk'), the idyll of Juan and Haidée is allowed to touch us with its paradisal innocence and youthful ardour:

> They were alone, but not alone as they
> Who shut in chambers think it loneliness.
> The silent ocean and the starlight bay,
> The twilight glow, which momently grew less,
> The voiceless sands and dropping caves, that lay
> Around them, made them to each other press,
> As if there were no life beneath the sky
> Save theirs, and that their life could never die.
>
> They feared no eyes nor ears on that lone beach,
> They felt no terrors from the night, they were
> All in all to each other. Though their speech
> Was broken words, they thought a language there,
> And all the burning tongues the passions teach
> Found in one sigh the best interpreter
> Of nature's oracle, first love, that all
> Which Eve has left her daughters since her fall.
>
> (Stanzas 188 and 189, page 149)

Haidée is a Rousseauesque construct, 'Nature's bride' and 'Passion's child', who is related to Eve in Eden yet handled with sufficient 'realism' to make her seem typical of any healthy young woman giving free rein to physical infatuation. The tenderness extended to her by Byron embraces also her pirate father, an ardent Greek patriot:

> The isle is now all desolate and bare,
> Its dwellings down, its tenants passed away;
> None but her own and father's grave is there,
> And nothing outward tells of human clay. . . .
>
> But many a Greek maid in loving song
> Sighs o'er her name; and many an islander
> With her sire's story makes the night less long.
> Valour was his, and beauty dwelt with her. . . .
>
> (Canto 4, Stanzas 72 and 73, page 207)

This is in effect a lament for the highest common factors in the values of Byron's 'Oriental' verse narratives – devotion in love, bravery in fight. Haidée and Lambro are 'Byronic' in conception, though 'Byronism' is modified by Juanist discourse. They are the most 'heroic' personages in *Don Juan*, almost meeting that 'uncommon want' of a hero which Byron expresses in the first stanza of his first canto.

But at a very different point in Juanism's range we find him sarcastically undermining the very idea of 'heroism', as conventionally conceived, when Juan participates in the siege of Ismail in Cantos 7 and 8. Byron's boisterous play with Russian surnames –

> . . . There were Strongenoff and Strokonoff,
> Meknop, Serge Lwow, Arseniew of modern Greece,
> And Tschitsshakoff and Roguenoff and Chokenoff
> And others of twelve consonants apiece. . . .
>
> (Canto 7, stanza 15, page 298)

– preludes full acknowledgement of the horrors of war, though violence in a just cause is not rejected, since 'revolution/Alone can save the earth from hell's pollution' (Canto 8, stanza 51, page 329). The account of the siege and ensuing sack mingles, perhaps unsuccessfully, exciting direct narrative, grimly ironic commentary and macabre detail reminiscent of *The Siege of Corinth* rendered with problematic jocularity:

> A dying Moslem, who had felt the foot
> Of a foe o'er him, snatched at it and bit
> The very tendon which is most acute
> (That which some ancient Muse or modern wit
> Named after thee, Achilles), and quite through't
> He made the teeth meet, nor relinquished it
> Even with his life, for (but they lie) 'tis said
> To the live leg still clung the severed head.
>
> (Canto 8, stanza 84, page 338)

If Byron can be excused here because he is using the story as the basis for a typical appeal to 'fact', to 'realism' against all kinds of 'lies', whether made in the interests of propaganda or mere sensationalism, his handling of the relative lack of rape attributed to the victorious Russians steps beyond what our present-day taste can accept:

> Some voices of the buxom middle-aged
> Were also heard to wonder in the din
> (Widows of forty were these birds long caged),
> 'Wherefore the ravishing did not begin?'

However, by the end of the stanza Byron himself, as if repenting his jest, expresses the hope that the women escaped (Canto 8, stanza 132, page 350). And this canto contains some of his most ringing denunciations of war and despotism.

The range of effects of which his stanza and his Juanist style were capable is demonstrated by the opening of Canto 9. Wellington, Britain's great martial hero, is genially abused in a mock dedication which suddenly moves from contemporary politics into three extraordinary stanzas which remind us that Byron was a compatriot of Macpherson of the rant (see p. 65), and displays directly the secular Calvinism which underlies, or overarches, the whole poem's sequence of human crimes and follies:

> Death laughs. Go ponder o'er the skeleton
> With which men image out the unknown thing
> That hides the past world, like to a set sun
> Which still elsewhere may rouse a brighter spring.
> Death laughs at all you weep for. Look upon
> This hourly dread of all, whose threatened sting
> Turns life to terror, even though in its sheath.
> Mark how its lipless mouth grins without breath!
>
> Mark how it laughs and scorns at all you are!
> And yet was what you are. From ear to ear
> It laughs not. There is now no fleshy bar
> So called. The Antic long hath ceased to hear,
> But still he smiles. And whether near or far
> He strips from man that mantle (far more dear
> Than even the tailor's), his incarnate skin,
> White, black, or copper – the dead bones will grin.
>
> And thus Death laughs. It is sad merriment,
> But still it is so; and with such example
> Why should not Life be equally content
> With his superior in a smile to trample
> Upon the nothings which are daily spent
> Like bubbles on an ocean much less ample
> Than the eternal deluge, which devours
> Suns as rays, worlds as atoms, years like hours?
>
> (Canto 9, stanzas 10–12, pages 355–6)

These stanzas echo old Talbot's speech in Shakespeare's *Henry VI Part One* upon the death of his son – 'Thou antick, death, which laugh'st us here to scorn ...' – and Byron is working in the old Christian tradition of the *vanitas* which made the skull a focus of contemplation, the tradition in which Hamlet's meditation on Yorick also stands. But the rhythmic effect in the second of these stanzas, with its staccato short sentences and stark monosyllabic rhymes, is wholly unexpected – at the other extreme from that of the third, which unwinds from its semi-colon a long sentence recalling in tone and imagery Canto 4 of *Childe Harold*. The passage displays extraordinary technical virtuosity. (Incidentally, I take 'so called', which might look like padding, to be a particularly terse jibe at Evangelical Christians, prone to speak of mortal flesh as a barrier between the soul and its heavenly home.)

Another surprise awaits us in Canto XI, where Juan, just outside London, is ambushed by four footpads and shoots one of them. We are given his obituary in a stanza which plays yet another variation on the poem's persisting theme, that conventional concepts of heroism are idiotic, but does so with surprising intimacy in 'flash' London slang of the lower and criminal classes:

> He from the world had cut off a great man,
> Who in his time had made heroic bustle.
> Who in a row like Tom could lead the van,
> Booze in the ken or at the spellken hustle?
> Who queer a flat? Who (spite of Bow Street's ban)
> On the high toby spice so flash the muzzle?
> Who on a lark with black-eyed Sal (his blowing)
> So prime, so swell, so nutty, and so knowing?
>
> (Canto 11, stanza 19, page 401)

In the 'English' cantos, Byron's delight in digression prevails to an extent which some readers find irritating. His subject is primarily 'high society'. A last quotation can lead us to the large question: granted that this may be, as Virginia Woolf averred, 'the most readable poem of its length ever written',[18] how highly, finally, can we rate it? Of 'society', Byron writes in Canto 14

> With much to excite, there's little to exalt,
> Nothing that speaks to all men and all times,
> A sort of varnish over every fault,
> A kind of commonplace even in their crimes . . .
>
> When we have made our love and gamed our gaming,
> Drest, voted, shone, and maybe something more;
> With dandies dined, heard senators declaiming,
> Seen beauties brought to market by the score,
> Sad rakes to sadder husbands chastely taming,
> There's little left but to be bored or bore. . . .
>
> (stanzas 16 and 18, page 475)

Was Byron fatally implicated despite himself in the trivial values of his class and time and is *Don Juan* a poem whose jests, railleries, lyrical effusions and cynical digressions stem from nothing better than its author's underlying boredom?

The late Helen Gardner, in 1958, summarized the purport of *Juan* thus:

> Although Byron's vision of man and the world is not very flattering to our self-esteem, or very conforting to our hopes, it is not discouraging. Man may not be a very noble animal, but he has his moments of glory, and life provides pleasures and satisfactions of many kinds. . . . For all its bursts of cynicism, savagery and melancholy, there is a fundamental good humour in *Don Juan* . . .

But she adds, 'wisdom of the highest kind Byron did not attain to, and this prevents him from ranking with the greatest poets.'[19] W. W. Robson, in his influential essay on 'Byron and Sincerity' (1966) is rather harsher. While conceding that *Juan* is a 'triumph of personality', he insists that the Byronic temperament disqualifies it from the highest slopes of Parnassus. 'Great art cannot be made out of a boredom with oneself, which is expressed as a boredom with one's subject matter.'[20]

You may agree with either, or both, of these judgements. You may furthermore feel, like so many readers before you, that Byron's vision not only lacks the highest qualities, but is, when all is said and done, anti-moral. George M. Ridenour, author of a stimulating book on *The Style of Don Juan*, concludes his preface cautiously:

> While I would like to think that people read and enjoy *Don Juan*, I would not like to think that they take it as exemplary . . . What I must perceive finally in *Don Juan* is a sophistication which (in highly debased form, to be sure) we have already too much of. *Don Juan* is, I think, a beautiful, exciting, touching, and rather terrifying vision of a personal and cultural dead end.[21]

According to Ridenour, Byron's cleverness is sterile. He's *too* clever to be 'exemplary', too 'sophisticated' to be of practical use as a moralist. Though intellectually much more coherent, Ridenour's position isn't so far from *Blackwood's*: the poem is 'beautiful' but ethically dubious. (Ridenour, however, calls Byron's vision 'honest, humane, and gallant', not 'depraved'.)

I'll now reason my own judgement by stages.

Robson and Gardner seem, in different ways, arbitrary in their criteria. It is not at all clear that 'great art' cannot be made from boredom with oneself; feelings akin to 'boredom' with 'self' are projected in Hamlet's soliloquies and in powerful novels by Tolstoy and Dostoevsky. Why, anyway, *should* the 'self' be regarded as other than 'boring'? 'Wisdom' is a Humpty-Dumpty word. It means, roughly, 'what I agree with'. The implicit comparison in Gardner's essay is almost certainly with Wordsworth. Well, the Wordsworth who wanted to see *Don Juan* knocked on the head without pretence of a fair review may seem to you no more 'wise' than the Byron who never forgave his bookish, bewildered young wife. You may feel, as Byron did, that Wordsworth can seem so secure in his 'wisdom' only because he ignores or mystifies matters like the bloodshed at Waterloo which Byron believed had to be confronted. In any case, 'greatness' and 'highness' aren't absolute qualities. They are relative, and time-bound. Some of Byron's older contemporaries believed till they died that Macpherson's *Ossian* was 'great' poetry. The 'greatness' of John Donne, which many now take as axiomatic, was eclipsed between the mid-seventeenth century and the early twentieth.

Another problem with 'greatness' relates to 'genre'. From the classical literary theorists the West inherited the notion that 'tragedy' and 'epic' were 'higher' than 'comedy', which resorted to 'low' subject-matter (that is, to the lives of ordinary people in everyday situations). Modern categories such as 'realism', 'modernism' and 'the absurd' have challenged neo-classical hierarchy in the arts. It is by no means as clear now as it seemed to be in 1819 that a funny, indignant poem informed by an atheistical and materialistic viewpoint is necessarily inferior to a solemn one about military heroism (epic), to one which endorses the judgements of fate (tragic), or to one which criticizes society from a clearly defined moral basis (satiric).

Byron's poetry has in fact been a very important influence on twentieth-century literature. Yeats admired and learnt from the conversational momentum of his syntax. It affected Eliot more than 'Old Possum' admitted, but W. H. Auden was happy to pay Byron the sincere compliment of extensive imitation. Virginia Woolf's admiration has been noted. An entire book has latterly been devoted to exploring affinities between *Juan* and that most important of all Modernist novels, James Joyce's *Ulysses*.[22]

But this seems to involve a distraction from the actual character of *Juan* as a work, and I would be no more happy with over-zealous emphasis on affinities (though some do exist) between Byron and such writers of self-consciously post-Modernist fiction as John Fowles and Salman Rushdie, with their intrusive authors. Such writing tends to query the reality of 'reality', to seek understanding through fantasy. And in Byron there is, after all, a dogged down-to-earthness, a conviction that the solid, if dangerous, world must be confronted 'as it really is'.

I've argued that Byron's address to us in *Don Juan* is akin to that of the 'realist' novelist. But clearly not *the same*. Whereas Fielding in *Tom Jones* could only take off classical epic in parodic prose, Byron can, either for ironic or 'serious' effect, produce lines which are 'Dantesque', 'Shakespearian', 'Miltonic', 'Augustan', and which briefly represent, rather than parody, these traditional 'high' discourses. His methods are different, again, from the brilliant play of discourses, comic and serious, sentimental and ironic, in Dicken's novels. To compare *Don Juan* with any other work in English poetry or fiction seems pointless. It is generically unique. *Don Juan* diverts us with a large range of discourses on the base of a stanza-form new to English and never handled with such assurance since. It could be said to define the very standards by which we can judge it. Of its kind, it is the best, and indeed truly the *only* example.

But ultimately, questions of 'value' in literature can't be subsumed under statements of literary-historical 'fact'. *Ossian*, likewise, was a unique construction. I'll leave you with a not-so-simple question. *If* the criterion of value in poetry is, as Ridenour and Gardner imply, ethical usefulness to its readers, does *Juan* now seem more or less useful than other poems, as we make the history of our own times? I love the poem for its champagne wit, but also for its consistent defence of what seem to me humane values – tolerance, anti-militarism and so on. But your answer may well depend on your gender. Granted that women reacted against *Juan* in Byron's lifetime, do their objections now seem to have any basis? Or are there perhaps new, present-day bases on which women should object to Byron's vision of humankind?

# Notes and References

**Chapter One**

1 A. D. Harvey, *English Poetry in a Changing Society 1780–1825*. (London, Alison and Busby: 1980) p. 115.
2 *Ibid.*, p. 101
3 P. W. Martin, *Byron: a poet before his public* (Cambridge University Press: 1982) pp. 31–39.
4 'The Widow's Tale' in *Tales, 1812 and other Selected Poems*, (ed. Howard Mills, Cambridge University Press: 1967) p. 201.
5 See, beside Mills's selection above, that by John Lucas (London, Longman: 1967).
6 W. Scott, *Poetical Works* (ed. J. L. Robertson, Oxford University Press: 1894) p. 13.
7 *Ibid.*, p. 52.
8 *Ibid.*, p. 165.
9 *Ibid*, pp. 233–4.
10 Martin, *op. cit.*, p. 44, in a book published in the 1980s, alleges that despite the attention which some critics have given them, 'the general quality of the poetry of the tales is so self-evidently poor that there is no longer any need to demonstrate this fact'.
11 Marilyn Butler, *Romantics, Rebels and Reactionaries: English Literature and its Background 1760–1830* (Oxford University Press: 1981) p. 141.
12 Byron, *Don Juan* (ed. T. Steffan *et al.*, London, Penguin: 1977 revised edition) p. 424.
13 Byron *Letters and Journals* (ed. L. A. Marchand, 12 vols, London, John Murray: 1973–82) Vol. 1, pp. 227–8.
14 A. Pushkin, *Letters* (ed. J. T. Shaw, Wisconsin, University of Wisconsin Press: 1967) Vol. 1, p. 213.
15 J. W. von Goethe, *Faust* (trans. B. Taylor, New York, Random House: 1950) p. 181.
16 Byron, *The Complete Poetical Works*, Vol. III, (ed. J. J. McGann, Oxford University Press: 1981) pp. 259–65.

17  T. L. Peacock, *Nightmare Abbey and Crotchet Castle* (London, Penguin: 1968 edn) pp. 99–100.
18  B. Russell, *History of Western Philosophy*, (London, Allen and Unwin: 1979) pp. 716–21.
19  Byron, *Complete Poetical Works*, Vol. III.
20  *The Works of Frederick Schiller: Early Dramas and Romances* (trans. H. G. Bohn, London, Bohn: 1850) p. 102.
21  Quoted in *Study Companion to Jane Eyre*, A 102 Arts Foundation Course, (Milton Keynes, Open University Press: 1978) p. 14.

## Chapter Two

1  Byron, *Complete Poetical Works*, Vol. III, p. 481.
2  Robert F. Gleckner, *Byron and the Ruins of Paradise*, (Baltimore, Johns Hopkins Press: 1967) p. 171.
3  Byron, *Complete Poetical Works*, Vol. III.
4  Bernard Blackstone, *Byron* Vol. I (London, British Council: 1970) p. 48.
5  Gleckner, *op. cit.*, pp. 191–2.

## Chapter Three

1  Thomas Moore, *Poetical Works* (London, Gall and Inglis: n.d.) pp. 189, 254.
2  Byron, *Complete Poetical Works*, Vol. III, p. 467.
3  Byron, *Letters and Journals*, Vol. 5 (ed. Leslie A. Marchand, London Murray, 1973–82) p. 176.
4  I am grateful to Dr Hamish Henderson, of the School of Scottish Studies, University of Edinburgh, for drawing this version to my attention and supplying the transcription. Her rendering can be heard on 'Up the Dee and doon the Don' (issued as an audiocassette LIFC 7001 by Lismor Recordings of Glasgow, 1984).
5  Louis Crompton, *Byron and Greek Love: Homophobia in Nineteenth-Century England*, (London, Faber: 1985) pp. 3, 8, 62, 301–11.
6  Stendhal, *Life of Rossini* (trans. R. N. Coe, London, Calder and Boyars: 1970) p. 3.
7  Leigh Hunt, *Lord Byron and Some of his Contemporaries* (London, Colburn: 1828) pp. 37–8.

## Chapter Four

1  Russell, *op. cit.*, p. 717.
2  Leslie A. Marchand, *Byron: A Portrait* (London, John Murray: 1971) pp. 13, 15.
3  E. P. Thompson, *The Making of the English Working Class*, (London, Gollancz: 1963) pp. 469–70.
4  Byron, *Letters and Journals*, Vol. 5, p. 149.
5  Byron, *Letters and Journals*, Vol. 7, p. 44.
6  Butler, *op. cit.*, pp. 138–40.

7 Thompson, *op. cit.* , pp. 722–3.
8 Byron, *Letters and Journals*, Vol. 6, p. 76.
9 Robert Southey, *Letters of Robert Southey: A Selection* (ed. M. H. Fitzgerald, Oxford University Press: 1901) p. 306.
10 Robert Southey, *Poetical Works* (London, Longman: 1844) p. 103.
11 *Ibid.*, pp. 771–85.
12 *Ibid.*, p. 769.
13 T. S. Eliot, *On Poetry and Poets*, (London, Faber: 1957) pp. 193–206.
14 Byron, *Don Juan* (ed. Steffan *et al.*) p. 379.
15 For further discussion of this, see Alan Bold, ed. *Byron: Wrath and Rhyme* (London, Vision Press, 1983).
16 Paul West, *Byron and the Spoiler's Art* (London, Chatto and Windus, 1960)
17 F. R. Leavis, *Revaluation* (London, Chatto and Windus: 1936) pp. 148–53.
18 Peter Vassallo, *Byron: The Italian Literary Influence* (London, Macmillan: 1984) discusses this debt, and others, in detail. The transmigration of literary influence between languages is a fascinating business. Pushkin developed his own elaborate Russian stanza form – fourteen lines rhyming *ababccddeffegg* – when he followed his idol Byron into the 'novel in verse' with his *Eugene Onegin*. An Indian, Vikram Seth, has latterly used this for a novel in English, *The Golden Gate* (London, Faber: 1986).
19 Blackstone, *op cit.*, Vol. 3, (1971) p. 51.
20 Matthew Arnold, *Poems* (ed. K. Allott, London, Longman: 1965) pp. 239 ff.
21 Burns' version, from *The Poems and Songs of Robert Burns*, Vol. I (ed. James Kinsley, Oxford University Press: 1968) p. 385.

## Chapter Five

1 *Blackwood's Magazine No. XXIX*, Vol. V. (Edinburgh: 1819) pp. 512–22.
2 Kelvin Everest, *Romantic Poetry, Units 9–10: The Historical Context and the Literary Scene* (Milton Keynes, Open University Press: 1984) pp. 18–20.
3 *Ibid.*
4 *Blackwood's, loc. cit.*
5 Byron, *Letters and Journals*, Vol. 8, pp. 11–12, Vol. 9, pp. 50–1.
6 *Ibid.*, Vol. 3, p. 220.
7 Byron, *Don Juan* (ed. Steffan *et al.*) p. 430.
8 *Byron's Don Juan: A Variorum Edition*, Vol. I (ed. T. G. Steffan and W. W. Pratt, University of Texas Press: 1957) pp. 16–23.
9 Andrew Rutherford, ed., *Byron: The Critical Heritage* (London, Routledge and Kegan Paul: 1970) pp. 159–78.
10 Byron, *Letters and Journals*, Vol. 8, p. 148.
11 Byron, *Don Juan* (ed. Steffan *et al.*) p. 9.
12 *Ibid.*, pp. 37–40.
13 Quoted in *ibid.*, 9–10.

14   *Byron's Don Juan: A Variorum Edition*, Vol. I, p. 341.
15   Byron, *Don Juan* (ed. T. Steffan *et al*., London, Penguin: 1977 revised edition.)
16   Jerome J. McGann, *Don Juan in Context* (London, John Murray: 1976) pp. 2, 4, 116–17, 128–31.
17   *Blackwood's, loc. cit.*, p. 552.
18   Quoted in McGann, *Don Juan in Context*, p. 10.
19   Helen Gardner, 'Don Juan' in *English Romantic Poets: Modern Essays in Criticism* (second edition, ed. M. H. Abrams, Oxford University Press: 1975) p. 311.
20   W. W. Robson, 'Byron and Sincerity' in *ibid*., p. 300.
21   George G. Ridenour, *The Style of Don Juan*, (New Haven, Yale University Press: 1960) pp. xii–xiii.
22   Hermione de Almeida, *Byron and Joyce Through Homer: Don Juan and Ulysses* (London, Macmillan: 1981).

# Further Reading

### Works by Byron

*Don Juan* can be read in full conveniently, and quite cheaply, in the Penguin edition by T. G. Steffan, E. Steffan and W. W. Pratt (most lately revised in 1982) and in *The Oxford Authors Byron* (Oxford University Press, 1986) edited by Jerome J. McGann, who claims to have superseded Steffan *et al*: this volume also contains a generous selection of other verse and prose.

Jerome J. McGann's edition of Byron's *Complete Poetical Works* in seven volumes (Oxford University Press, 1980–, still not complete) certainly replaces all others. Unfortunately, the only *Poetical Works* more or less complete in one paperback volume is the nasty 'Oxford Standard' first edited by Frederick Page in 1904, revised by John Jump in 1970, with its double columns of small print. (Oxford University Press)

The complete *Letters and Journals* have been edited by Leslie A. Marchand in 12 volumes (John Murray, 1973–82). Marchand's paperback selection from these is available.

## Works about Byron

### Biographical

Leslie A. Marchand, again, is the author of the definitive *Byron: A Biography* in three volumes (Murray, 1957) and of an abridgement, with some revisions, *Byron: A Portrait* (Murray, 1971). There are of course a very large number of other biographical studies. Among these may be mentioned Iris Origo's *The Last Attachment* (1949), Doris Langley Moore's *The Late Lord Byron* (1961) and *Lord Byron: Accounts Rendered* (1974), John Buxton's *Byron and Shelley* (1968) and Louis Crompton's *Byron and Greek Love* (1985) – the last a study of Byron's homosexuality.

### Critical works

Collections of critical views can be found in *Byron: The Critical Heritage*, edited by Andrew Rutherford (Routledge, 1970) which contains contemporary and Victorian judgements, in Paul West (ed) *Byron* (Prentice-Hall 1963) and in John Jump (ed.) *'Childe Harold's Pilgrimage' and 'Don Juan': A Casebook* (Macmillan, 1973). I now list a selection of important studies. Those marked with an asterisk have chapters or single essays on Byron.

*M. Abrams, ed. *English Romantic Poets* (Oxford University Press, 1975).

Alan Bold, ed. *Byron: Wrath and Rhyme* (Vision Press, 1983).

Michael Cooke, *The Blind Man Traces the Circle* (Princeton University Press, 1969).

*Michael Cooke, *Acts of Inclusion: Studies Bearing on an Elementary Theory of Romanticism* (Yale University Press, 1979).

*T. S. Eliot, *On Poetry and Poets* (Faber, 1957).

Robert F. Gleckner, *Byron and the Ruins of Paradise* (Johns Hopkins Press, 1967).

*Karl Kroeber, *Romantic Narrative Art* (University of Wisconsin Press, 1960).

*F. R. Leavis, *Revaluation* (Chatto and Windus, 1936).

P. W. Martin, *Byron: A Poet Before His Public* (Cambridge University Press, 1982).

Jerome J. McGann, *Fiery Dust: Byron's Poetic Development* (University of Chicago Press, 1968.

*Jerome J. McGann, Don Juan in Context* (John Murray, 1976).

*W. W. Robson, *Critical Essays* (Routledge and Kegan Paul, 1966).

George M. Ridenour, *The Style of Don Juan* (Yale University Press, 1960).

Andrew Rutherford, *Byron: A Critical Study* (Oliver and Boyd, 1961).

Peter Vassallo, *Byron: The Italian Literary Influence* (Macmillan, 1984).

Paul West, *Byron and the Spoiler's Art* (Chatto and Windus, 1960).

# Index

18, 20, 22; 'Ode to
Napoleon Bonaparte',
14–16; 'One struggle
more', 42–43; *Prisoner of
Chillon, The*, 28–36, 37;
'Remember thee', 41–42;
'She walks in beauty',
38–40; *Siege of Corinth,
The*, 8, 24–28, 31, 32, 37,
83; 'Sonnet on Chillon',
29–30; 'The spell if broke',
41–42; 'So we'll go no
more a roving', 40–1;
'Stanzas to Augusta', 43;
'To the Author of a
Sonnet', 41; 'to Thomas
Moore', 41; *Vision of
Judgement, The*, 48, 49ff;
'Written after Swimming',
41.

Campbell, Thomas, 1, 76
Castlereagh, Lord, 42, 53, 69
Chaucer, Geoffrey, 35, 71
Churchill, Charles, 41, 70
Clairmont, Claire, 52
Coleridge, Samuel Taylor, 1, 2,
4, 5, 6, 27, 30, 33–34, 35,
51–52, 76
Constable, ARchibald, 2
Crabbe, George, 1, 2, 3–4, 9
Crompton, Louis, 42
Cruickshank, George, 19

Dante Alighieri, 28, 38, 48, 88
Dickens, Charles, 59, 88
Donne, John, 87
Dostoevsky, Fryodor, 63, 86
Dunbar, William, 57

Eastlake, Lady, 22
Eastwood, Clint, 22
*Edinburgh Review*, 23
Edleston, John, 42

Eliot, T.S., 56–58, 87
Everest, Kelvin, 68

Fielding, Henry, 3, 59, 69–70,
75, 87
Fleming, Ian, 10
Fox, C.J., 63

Gardner, Helen, 86
George III, 53, 60ff
Gibbon, Edward, 17, 29, 48, 67
Gifford, William, 26
Gleckner, Robert F., 26, 30
Goethe, J.W.von, 13–14, 17,
21, 22, 73
Gogol, Nikolai, 63
Grattan, Henry, 51
Greece *see under Byron*
Guiccioli, Countess, 72

Harvey, A.D., 1
Hitler, Adolf, 14
Hobhouse, J.C., 43, 50, 71
Hunt, John, 72
Hunt, Leigh, 48, 51, 56, 60, 72

Jefferson, Thomas, 68
Joyce, James, 87
'Junius', 55, 63

Keats, John, 2, 3, 56, 57, 72
Kinnaird, Douglas, 38
Laclos, Choderlos de, 69–70,
75
Leavis, F.R., 58–59, 62
Lennon, John, 16
Lermontov, M.Y., 23
Lochart, J.G., 65
Longman, 2
Luddism, 50, 67, 71

Macaulay, T.B., 49
McGann, J.J. 24, 25, 43, 80–81
Mackenzie, Henry, 21